DaddyHoot

DaddyHoot

The Lighter Side of Fatherhood

by

Margaret G. Bigger

Author of *MotherHoot*

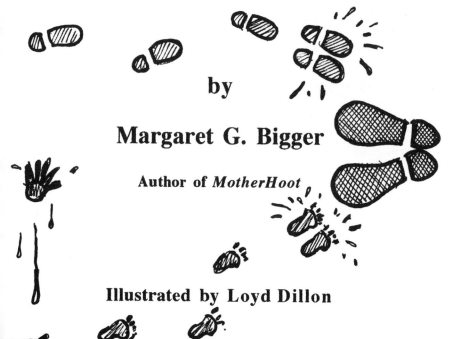

Illustrated by Loyd Dillon

ABB   A. Borough Books

ISBN 0-9640606-9-8

Library of Congress Catalog Card Number: 2001 132057

Printed in the United States of America

Cover design by Loyd Dillon
Illustrations by Loyd Dillon

ABB

A. Borough Books
P.O. Box 15391
Charlotte NC 28211

CONTENTS

Contributors

Kathy Almond
Bet Ancrum
Ashley Anderson
Bill Anthony
Sally Aycock
Delores Banner
Dana Bates
Trick Beamer
Randy Bigger
Valerie Bittner
Susan Blanton
Samantha Boergert
A. Fran Booth
Jean Brebner
Pat Brooks
Frank Brown
Martha M. Bullen
Annette Burkhard
Michelle Byrd
C. S. Cannon
Marian Carlsson
Elise Carter
Beverly Cassels
Penn Cassels
George Caylor
Joy Christenbury
Sarah Clardy
Alan Clark
Bill Clark
Chris Clemente
Maria Cline
Mary Lisi Collins
Andrea Cooper
Carmen Covington-Davis
Jim Covington
Ned Crandall
Robert Craig, Jr.
Kenneth Crummit
Dick Daniels
Mary B. Davis
Bill Deweese
Loyd Dillon
Harriet Dolin
Leslie Duncan
Robbye Dunning
Sue Elrod
Patrick Evans
Bonnie Famolari
Bernie Fiss
Wendy Foley
David Foltz
Leighton Ford
Bill Foster
Linda Fowler

David Friese
Alice Froelich
Michelle Futch
Judy Gaines
Ted Garner
Nora Geddie
Lish Gennett
Anne Glenn
Carol Goldsborough
Meredith Granger
John Greig
Chuck Hahn
Cleta Hamer
Mark Haze
Monica Henderson
Fred Hodges
Amy Holthouser
Theresa Horne
Emily Horton
Lisa Hutchinson
Brian Howard
David Jennings
Doug Johnson
George Johnston
Allan Jolly
Judith Justice
Annelle Kelly
Jeff Kelly
Shirley Kennedy
Robin Kirby
Sara Kratt
Thelma Kube
Pam Lapato
Barbara Larson
Darrell Laurant
Jarvis Lessane
Joe Leyland
Jeanne Livesay
David Long
Libby Lum
Greg Marshall
Rick Mazich
Katherine McAdams
Nancy McCall
Loonis McGlohon
Dixon McGuire
Ethel McMillan
Julie A. Menley
Christina Metze
Nan Millette
James Miller
Dianne Mills
Jo Minchew

Edward Mitchell
Mike Mizak
Beth Mlady
Bobbie Moore
Sue Morton
Kathy Moss
Darlene Mullis
Lisa Munsey
Meredith Murry
Marlene M. Nice
Athena Nicolas
Janet Noble
Thomas L. Odom
Dean Ogden
Harriet Orth
Nan Patrick
Bill Pearce
Bill Perry
Jeff Pinkston
Tom Powell
Karen Powers
Cindy Quayle
John Quinn
T.J. Quinn
Ahmed Radi
Tareq Radi
Donna Reed
Andy Rent
Jordan Rich
Mike Roberts
Tom Rogers
Janet Rose
Amy Sangston
Keith Shannon
Betty Simpson
Mitch Simpson
Sherri Smith
Lori Sondov
Katheryn Sonner
Becky Staton
Gerald Stone
Russell Strosnider
Ralph Terry
Branko Terzic
Greg Thompson
Chappie Thrift
Scott Vallandingham
Aldo Vandermolen
Bernie Varska
Maria Weed
Dana White
Steve Wilson
Mike Wittman
Linda Zinkann

& thanks to:

KKVV
Las Vegas NV

KLPW
Washington MO

KPRC
Houston TX

WBZ
Boston MA

WCCF
Punta Gorda FL

WCUZ
Grand Rapids MI

WKZO
Kalamazoo MI

WLNI
Lynchburg, VA

WLSQ
Roanoke VA

WONU
Bourbonnais IL

WRVX
Lynchburg VA

WWSR
St. Albans VT

WYUU
St. Petersburg FL

Erskine Overnight

INTRODUCTION

A daddy is not just a father. He may not even be a biological father. He's loving and loveable. He loves laughing, but he's laughable, too!

That what this book is about: daddies who can see the humor in situations with their kids—even if it takes a few years.

DaddyHoot, I hope, will also give new fathers a view of what's ahead and seasoned dads a sense of humor to carry them through. When you see what other pops have put up with, your current crisis may seem comical.

Folks, you can't make up stuff like this! Since 1991, I've been collecting true humorous stories about engagements, weddings, honeymoons, "senior humor" experiences, motherhood and now fatherhood and grandfatherhood. If I tried to put these tales in a fiction book, readers would roll their eyes and say, "Oh, Margaret, REALLY!"

Or would they? A novelist I know made an observation, "Some of those stories would never see the light of day. Your editor would have cut them out as 'unbelieveable.'"

Don't believe me? Check out the chapter called "Did What?"

Fathers, mothers and children: this is a pick-me-up book. Not to be read straight through in one sitting, it's one you can pick up and put down whenever you need that little "lift."

It's a celebration of fatherhood, a tribute to daddies everywhere.

WHO'S PREGNANT? WE ARE!

Some people think only women have preliminary jitters, pregnancy pains and birthing stories. Wrong!

Aaron attended a birthing class with his wife, Amy. A bit dubious at first, he learned a lot. He soon discovered that the teacher was right when she said, "Pregnancy lasts eight months and then a year."

Expectations

For various medical reasons, Miriam's doctor thought she was further along than she was. He also couldn't hear a heartbeat, so he ordered an x-ray.

When she dropped the negative into place, the x-ray technician let out an unprofessional "Oh, my God!"

Jeff, the expectant dad, envisioned a monster. He took a look. There were unmistakably three bodies. Naturally, the physician recommended more specialized care. He told them to return every four weeks for a sonogram.

Four weeks later, Jeff and Miriam were back in his office for the sonogram. It showed quads.

"We're not coming back for any more tests!" they declared.

Pregnancy pains and more—male version.

"It's time!" gasped the mom-in-labor from a gurney.

Dad jumped up, slipped down, conked his head and split it open.

He got to the operating room before she did.

When Mama Leslie was growing with twins, Daddy Matt was growing, too. A photograph proved it.
How come?
When Leslie drank extra milk, Matt did, too. When Mama ate "pregnant food" for two, Daddy did, too.

Maria woke up suddenly one night in their apartment in Fargo, North Dakota, when her husband Don was in grad school. Don is hard to wake up, so she had to punch him a few times. "I'm having contractions! I need for you to time them. The clock is on your side," she said.
"Now!" she said, as another one hit her. Each time, she let him know when it started and ended.
Don started calling out numbers that didn't mean anything. Then she realized that her statistician husband was repeating formulas in his sleep.

It was a rotten day in Richmond. This Virginia city seldom has a snowfall, much less a blizzard with 20 inches on the ground.
To brighten the morning, Steve offered to cook breakfast for Laura, nine months pregnant, and 4-year-old Taylor. The first two sets of pancakes he burned. The third ones were gooey. Laura politely picked at them, but Taylor refused to eat. He wanted to play outside, but the storm was too fierce.
A short while later, Laura began feeling as though she had morning sickness all over again. Just a few minutes after she grew ill, Steve began flu-like symptoms. Between throwups, Laura called her mother to come pick up Taylor before he caught their illness.
Mom's car was the only one on the road, but it still took her an hour to go five miles. Soon after she had left with Taylor, Laura called her doctor.
"You mustn't get dehydrated," he warned. "Better come to the hospital."
Poor Mom. Once home, she had to creep back between the snowdrifts to transport Laura—and Steve—to the hospital.

Much to her shock Laura had been too sick to notice that she was in full labor. But Steve was equally ill. Was he in labor too? No. Like Laura, he had salmonella poisoning from the pancake batter's raw eggs.

Heidi's husband admitted to co-workers that he had a "thing" about her water breaking. Her baby was due in April, and in March he had already placed plastic on the rugs and sofa. He kept towels in the car for the uncertain emergency.

In early April, Heidi was talking with her mother on the phone, "Oh no!" she said in a near shout. "My water broke!"

Hubby rushed in with every towel from the bathroom. She dropped the phone. "April Fool!"

In telling about the merciless trick she had played on him that morning, he simply couldn't understand why his colleagues were snickering.

On the topic of pregnancy, a MotherHoot Tip for Sanity is: "Forgive your hubby, no matter what he says or does; you may need him later." Here are some of the reasons this tip can save marriages.

Preparing to go out, Cindy of Zephyrhills, Florida turned to her husband, "Do I look all right?"

"Yes."

Later, they were in a department store, where they had shopped for quite awhile. Cindy tried to put her hands in her pocket. What was wrong? Her maternity shorts were wrong side out—pockets hanging, seams showing, elastic front flapping. Cindy was mortified. "Why did you say I looked okay?"

Hubby was sheepish. "I didn't look at you."

Nan overheard her husband, Phil, talking on the phone one night. "Well sure I could," he said. "My wife is expecting twins early in the new year, but once she has them, we would be ready to move. England sounds wonderful!"

11

At a well-known restaurant in Connecticut, the young couple stopped for lunch during a vacation. Dixon and Frank had just finished the meal, when Dixon headed for the ladies room and Frank got up to pay the bill. After taking only a few steps, Dixon blacked out. The maitre d' and a waiter rushed to pick her up. Hubby helped the others drag her outside for air.

Bad plan. At the entrance, she got sick, a poor advertisement for their business. Management personnel were profuse with apologies and amends. They returned Frank's money for the food. They insisted on "doing something" for Dixon's comfort, bowing and scraping all the while. Dixon settled for tea and saltine crackers in the bar. At last, she felt well enough to walk, and they got up to leave.

It was then that Frank made the foot-in-mouth statement of their lifetimes. "It's okay," he told the manager. "She's pregnant. She does this all the time."

Why women lose self-esteem when pregnant:

As Sara was trying to get off the couch, Russell couldn't resist saying : "You look like a turtle trying to get up."

Toby's comment to Tuppins: "You look like a VW bug when you lie on your back."

Carl was astounded at the size of Cyndi's maternity panties. "When you're through with those," he remarked, "I'm going to use them for a car cover."

Ready, set, GO!

Lynne punched her husband, Fred, who was asleep next to her. "My water broke!"

Fred grumbled. "Go back to sleep. I'll call the plumber in the morning."

"Honey, it's time!" Deborah said, waking her husband. Already dressed in sweatpants and a top, he grabbed his cap and keys, ran out the door, hopped into the car and backed down the driveway.

Deborah was still inside the house.

The actual event.

Moms don't forget comments like these, either:

Pam was having her third C-section. "Just put a zipper in," her husband Nick told the doctor.

Brad's wife, Janet, was self-conscious about the squared-off shape of her feet. She even wore socks in the delivery room. Meanwhile, everything else was out for the world to see.

Brad, who often teased her about her ugly extremities was suddenly saying, "I was just kidding. I *love* your feet."

Some time later, he saw his daughter appear and exclaimed, "She's beautiful! She has my feet!"

Dads don't forget moments like these:

The pain in Sean's belly was intense. Trina was in hard labor, but *he* was hurting

As Trina leaned forward, following instructions to push with all her might, she buried her face against Sean. "I thought I was biting down on my husband's shirt," she recalled.

Well, it wasn't just his shirt. Sean's belly had a black and blue mark twice the size of a fist.

When he was told "You have a boy!" John was not surprised. After having seen the obvious appendage on the ultrasound, he and Leilani had named their son Jonathan.

Later, he observed Jonathan with a blue anklet lying in a nursery crib marked "baby boy."

But a girl was brought to Leilani's room for a feeding. Of course, John accused the Pennsylvania hospital of switching babies. A DNA test at an independent lab was ordered.

After an anguished period of time, the DNA verified that Jonathan was indeed their daughter. Oops!

"Bonnie, we have a son!" cried John, as he watched his child being born.

The doctor looked at him sorta funny. "No, you don't. It's a girl."

Soon after Keary woke up on a Sunday morning, she urged her husband, Xiao Qing, to take her to the hospital. The doctor sent them back home. She was not ready to deliver, he said.

At 10:28 that morning, while Keary was taking a bath, baby Evan made his presence known. Dad dialed 911 and tried to help Keary follow the dispatcher's instructions. Just as he was lifting his dripping son out of the water, five paramedics walked in to transport Keary to the hospital.

The biggest shock came later, when the insurance company refused to pay the hospital bill. Their reasons:

1.) The doctor didn't submit a bill for the delivery.

2.) The procedure was not pre-approved by their insurance plan.

Who? Why?

Alex's Atlanta business associate, Mike, named his first son Sam after Mike's father. When his wife Diana gave birth to a daughter, they named her Ella.

"It still catches me off-guard," says Alex's wife, Fran, "when, at firm picnics, I hear Mike calling for his children. Everyone stops eating for a moment and looks up, as his voice echoes through the air: 'Sam 'n Ella! Sam 'n Ella! Where are you?'"

Fran says it sounds like "a culinary red alert."

Why don't parents consider how other kids might tease their child? One little fellow in Missouri named Tom was kidded unmercifully. Why? His last name was Thumb.

Friends in both North Carolina and Virginia have told us about fraternal twins named Adam and Eve.

Probably the most amazing naming story was told me by a country woman many years ago. People in her neck of the woods thought it quite classy to give a child, male or female, a French-sounding name beginning with "La."
But a father was really furious when he came home from World War II to find out that his wife had named their daughter Latrine!

Some dads have trouble with names.

They had almost settled on their baby's name. Just before leaving the hospital, Mother had to fill in the birth certificate. Pen in hand, she asked, "Linda with an i or y?"
Her left-brained architect husband shrugged. "Both have an i."
Upon being shown the two spellings under consideration, the new dad raced out the door to a jewelry store. He had ordered a gold charm for his wife's bracelet which had their daughter's name spelled "Lyndia."

15

NEW POP, NEW BABE,
NO INSTRUCTIONS

How-to-manuals should come with infants. Ignorance is not bliss; it's terror. But some dads seem to catch on faster than others.

Their infant was screaming but wouldn't take his bottle. Jeanne was too sick to nurse him, but Stan got a great idea. He donned her familiar bathrobe to fool his son into thinking he was Mom.
Didn't work.

Just a few nights after their baby came home, Roy and his wife, Bobbie, switched roles for the wee-hours feeding. Roy gallantly offered to let her sleep.
But Bobbie couldn't sleep, waiting for him to return to bed. Concerned, she got up to check on him. There he was, groggily warming a Pepsi bottle.

His own son Kenneth said about his father a few years later: "He can gut a deer but can't change a diaper."

Michelle was holding her firstborn John high above her head, looking into his tiny eyes and "ooohing" and "aaahing" like silly new mommies do.
With that, John threw up—bull's-eye, right into her mouth. Billy, silly daddy, thought it was funny.

When Mitch's firstborn, Andrew, was born Thanksgiving weekend, he and Betty became the typical germ-paranoid parents. In fact, although Mitch was a minister, they did not take Andrew to church until January.

On his first visit, they raced into the parking lot with their precious bundle, stopped right in front of the nursery door and ran inside.

Thirty minutes later, during the sermon, a nursery worker looked out the window and asked, "Isn't that the pastor's car sitting in the middle of the parking lot with the engine running and two of the doors standing open?"

Mitch's perspective on germs changed a bit.

With Andrew, neither he nor Betty took him out of the house for a month after his birth.

With Aaron, they didn't take him out for a week.

With Ellie, they stopped at the mall on the way home from the hospital.

What is it about little girls? As is true of most new parents, Woody and his wife Anne kept their first two newborns, both boys, home initially. But when their daughter was born, Woody stopped by his office to show her off.

Dick, a first-time dad from New Jersey, took Randy out for a walk in the snow. Okay, Daddy walked; the bundled 1-year-old rode on a sled.

When they returned home, Randy and his snowsuit were soaking wet. "What happened?" Mom wanted to know.

Dick looked sheepish. With some prodding, he admitted that he had turned around to speak to his son and saw an empty sled. Back-tracking, he had found two wiggling feet sticking out of a snowdrift.

A Florida father, Chris, was telling me how his son, Anthony, 1, looks to his mom for permission to move on when he's crawling. Mom's "no" means no, and he stops instantly.

17

Dad's "no," however, has no effect at all. "I've tried to use the same tone of voice she does," said Chris, "but it still doesn't work. So I'm going to record her voice saying 'no,' so I can use it when she's away."

Dick from Salem, Virginia, confessed a "huge error" he'd made with his young son, John William, who was getting used to drinking from a cup with no top. He liked the "twirly-curly" straw, but he could be a little messy.

Dick had shown him how to suck up his spills with the cute straw. That, of course, was much more fun than drinking from the cup, so John William would pour out his milk and "schluurp!"

TERRIBLE—BUT BEARABLE—TWOS

Until your child is 2, you can't imagine what other parents were complaining about. But then, you just have to keep reminding yourself to keep a sense of humor.

Vacation. At their Myrtle Beach motel, the entire family was savoring the view from a balcony—everyone except Melinda, 2. Suddenly, Melinda locked the sliding glass door from the inside. Trapped: Mama, Daddy, grandparents, an aunt and Melinda's older sister.

They tried to talk her into flipping the lock. Then they yelled "Help!" to the sunbathers around the pool below.

Daddy Greg would handle this situation. He got mad and bellowed at her.

Melinda ran crying to the bathroom.

Jerry and Sue had been in their beautiful new home in Mount Pleasant, North Carolina for four days. After supper, Jerry took their son Justin, 6, upstairs for some father-son time. Their 2-year-old daughters, Anna and Shelley, stayed with their mother in the kitchen until she said, "Go upstairs and tell Daddy to give you a bath."

Soon Sue heard Justin laughing and the bath water running. The sound was coming from the master bath which had a garden tub. She assumed Jerry was giving all three a bath in the large tub.

Fifteen minutes later she went upstairs. Jerry and their son were locked in Justin's room for privacy. The twins were floating on top of overflowing water in the big tub, having a grand time. The water was still running—out of the tub, throughout the bathroom, into the master bedroom, down the hall and into the spare room. When Sue went downstairs to get the shop vac, she saw water dripping from the recessed ceiling lights.

House repairs, including a replaced ceiling and carpets, cost $18,000, a lot of time, trouble and tribulation. Needless to say, Jerry and Sue were the talk of the town.

Now, here's Jerry's side of the story:

His daughters poked their heads into Justin's room to say "Bath time!"

Jerry said, "Get your mommy to do it," and locked the door.

One Saturday morning in Kalamazoo, friends were knocking at Don's front door. No, banging on the door. Pounding. Don came bounding down the stairs in his underwear. The friends had stopped by to see if the family wanted to go out for breakfast. Then they had seen Don's toddler, Josh, through the window next to the door. His face and body were splattered with blood—or so they thought. They were banging to save his son's life.

Don recognized the red right off. Josh had been mixing a powdered fruit drink in the living room. Most of it was on him or the carpet.

Trumbull, who used to race cars, has a bad temper and vents it on the road.

His son Brian had heard him use his favorite bad word one too many times.

The 2-year-old jumped up on his pew at church and blasted the congregation with a vehement "Truck!"

"Whew!" said Trumbull.

Will was sitting in his high chair at the breakfast table next to a window in his San Antonio home.

A quick glance later, Daddy Bill heard himself saying, "Will! Don't blow your nose on the curtain."

It's the year of the pot.

In a Roanoke, Virginia, baby superstore, Dick was looking for something and didn't see that little Maggie had found a very comfortable, handy potty seat—and used it!

What did Dad do? Maggie had proudly performed as programmed; he couldn't scold her. Dick looked around. So far, no one had noticed. "So I snuck it out, rinsed if off, put it back and nobody knew," he said.

"A dog potty-trained my son," claimed Darren from Vermont. "We had tried everything: Cheerios in the toilet..."

"What?" I asked.

"You know, so he could aim for them. And we got those little toys that swell up when wet. Nothing worked."

Dale was 3, and he still hadn't gotten the idea. That is, until he watched Ginger, whom Darren describes as "our 90-pound-roll-across-lap-dog." Darren put Dale's potty chair outside with the dog, and he used it. Every day, they brought the chair closer to the house until Dale was ready to come inside.

David took his son, Greg, to a swimming pool. He was explaining that Greg should not urinate in his bathing suit or in the pool. The next thing he knew, Greg was using a nearby drain surrounded by a spider web.

Greg looked up. "The spiders aren't going to like that."

So how come Mike took his 2-year-old squirrel-hunting anyway? This Virginia dad was supposed to be baby-sitting. Guess this was his idea of "killing two birds with one stone."

No doubt, he'll never do that again. He was holding little Michael in one arm and tried shooting with the other hand. Kaboom! Michael wet him.*

* After this tale appeared in *MEN!*, Mike proudly explained his reasoning: "She never asked me to baby-sit again!"

You find out what it's like to be the father of a 2-year-old when...

* You can't find your car keys.

* You wake up to find him roaming, having left a trail of baby powder, toys, household items and toilet paper.

* Your shaving cream becomes decorative white paint for the floor, the cabinets, the wall and, of course, the baby.

* No crib sides, kiddie gate, dead bolt or chloroform will keep him in.

* The whine button turns on and the broken record bellows the "no" tune.

* Your other children try whining to get their way.

* Your extended family stops visiting.

* Your friends invite you to "adults only" parties.

* You wake up to the fact that she is saying "umbrella" while the rest of the family is still calling it a "bum-bum."

* You keep those damp baby wipes on hand FOR YOURSELF.

SAID *WHAT?*

We could hardly wait for them to talk. Then we couldn't shut them up. But wasn't it fun when they were learning new words?

"Dadada" was not a real word to Andrew, no matter how much Alvin, his dad, wished it were. Although he frequently babbled that sound, Andrew never looked at Alvin when he said it. His actual first word was "Bob."
Alvin's nickname? Andrew's grandfather's?
Nope.
When he said it, Andrew was reaching up to Bob, the kindly cook at the day care center.

Laurel was sitting in her high chair at breakfast when her face brightened with a new realization. "Oooo," she said pointing to herself. "Loorel." Her little finger turned to Andrea, her mother, "Mommy," and then to her dad, Alan, "Dummy."

David knew immediately that they should change a family habit, when their firstborn's first word was "Hardee's!"

Ellie has two older brothers. That, according to her parents, is why her first sentence was "Go away."

"These are not shoes," the salesman had told Ben, 2, as he was trying on some tennis shoes. "These are Reeboks."
That explains Ben's new word when he was playing in the tub with two trick-or-treat buckets on his feet: "Look! Reebuckets!"

Sometimes they surprise us...

David and Barbara were driving near their South Carolina home just before Easter when their son Jon, who was 4, cried out. "Mom! Dad! They were wrong!" He pointed to three wooden crosses near a church. "Jesus died in Rock Hill, South Carolina!"

amuse us...

Driving his son to an appointment in the Philly area, Ahmed was frustrated. Everything was going against them.

Tareq was enumerating their problems. "It's rainy," he grumbled. "All this traffic..."

"Be positive, son," Ahmed admonished, trying to think that way himself.

"I AM positive," he retorted glumly. "Positive we aren't going to get there."

While watching a football game with his father, Wes, 4, was fascinated with the color guard standing at attention during the singing of the "Star Spangled Banner."

"What are the guys with the guns there for?" he wondered aloud. "To shoot people who don't sing?"

Right after bath time, Rick of Fleetwood, Pennsylvania asked his daughter Maria if her nose were shiny and bright.

"No," said Maria. "My batteries are run down."

Her favorite stuffed animal was Rudolph, whose nose lit up when its ear was squeezed.

befuddle us...

Even at 7, Andrea from Pennsylvania, had an impressive vocabulary.

One evening at dinner, she announced, "I was sent to

the proctologist today."

Marlene and Dennis stopped eating and stared.

Dennis raised his eyebrows. "The school has a proctologist? What was this for?"

Andrea explained that she was being tested for the school's gifted and talented program. Her appointment had been with the school psychologist.

Larry was thinking about moving his family to Sarasota. But he didn't want his boss or co-workers to get wind of his idea.

He told his 5-year-old son but swore him to secrecy.

"I don't know why," said Rob. "I've had a cherry soda before."

"My daddy has a beard," announced Jonathan, 7.

An adult friend who knew David, his father, gave him an odd look. "No, he doesn't."

"Yes, he does," said Jonathan. "He shaves it off every day."

yes, and frustrate us!

Mother had bought Dad a shirt, tie and handkerchiefs for Father's Day and made Vivian promise that she wouldn't tell him about the gift.

When he came home that evening, Vivian ran to the door crying. "Guess what, Daddy! For Father's Day, you're getting no shirt, no tie and no handkerchiefs."

Rob and Kay gave their neighbors a vacation by adding two kids to their own for a total of four on a car trip from just outside Indianapolis to Florida.

On a rural road in Georgia, Kay made a comment from the front seat to their son Bob and was met by silence. Oh, oh.

Their 6-year-old must still be at that little gas station 50 miles back! Rob turned the car around while Mama Kay fretted about her poor little boy crying his eyes out to a policeman.

When they drove up at the service station, there sat Bob in the dirt with $6 worth of candy, munching away. "Go on," he said, "I'm not through yet."

When their four boys ranged in age from 5 to 8, Bob and his wife, Nancy, decided that it was time to teach them what to do in case of emergency. Bob sat the boys down and explained what constituted an emergency and told them to call 911. Then he and Nancy let them each practice on an unplugged telephone.

Later, they heard Daniel, 7, tell his grandmother what he had learned. "When there's an emergency, you run to the window, throw it open and yell, 'Nine, one, one!'"

Just who is this guy?

Clare's dad had shaved off his moustache. Little Clare wandered into her parent's bedroom early while they were still half asleep. She pulled on her mom's arm. "Is that our father?"
Her mother smiled. "I hope so."

When T. J. was in kindergarten, his mom thought he should know his father's name. Such information would be important in an emergency.
"What's Daddy's name?"
"Daddy."
"What does Mommy call him?"
"Hon."
"What does Uncle Chris call him?"
"Dummy."
"What does grandmother call Daddy?"
T.J. assumed a gruff voice, "Timothy Fay!"

Their daughter Sandra was taking a bath and needed help. Cleta was busy, so she nodded to her husband. "Your father will help you," she said.

"Is that my father?" Sandra wanted to know.

Cleta was taken aback until she realized that Sandra had always called George "Daddy."

Because his parents were separated shortly after his birth, Markale did not see his father, Mario, until they were reunited when he was 5 years old.

After meeting Mario at his grandmother Donna's house, Markale anxiously tried to explain to his mother how the visit went. Not quite sure of the reaction he was getting, he gave her a questioning look. "Mommy, do you know my daddy?"

How come...?

On a spring day, a driver pulled out in front of her dad's car and Morgan, 3, yelled out the window, "You stupid jerk!"

David, her father, couldn't get too mad, because she was repeating his exact words from another day.

But that had happened on an early spring day when his car window was up.

While his wife was at work, Michael was baby-sitting with Kira, 2. She was pretending to talk to her boyfriend from preschool on her plastic phone.

This California dad stepped to the doorway to hear her say in a dreamy voice, "That's right. I'm naked."

When Kira's mom came home, he was quick to repeat the quote and ask, "And where did your daughter get *that* idea?"

Matt, 5, of West Chester, Pennsylvania, eagerly tore into his birthday present from his visiting uncle. He was elated to find the large plastic robot he'd been wanting for weeks.

"Oh, I love this!" he gushed, not taking his eyes off the fantastic-looking figure. "I love it as much as Mom loves me and Dad loves his new car!"

One December Sunday morning, Martin's wife Martha and two children were in church while Martin was home washing his car. During the service, the minister called the youngsters up to the chancel and asked them what they were hoping to get for Christmas. Several boys and girls called out their choices: "A Nintendo!" "Barbie!" "Legos!"

Stuart, 6, who, like his father Martin is a sports car buff, spoke up, "I want a Ferrari!"

Daddy saw that he got one, too. A *kid*-size toy.

Blake, 3, from East Bridgewater, Massachusetts, had clicked into her Blues Clues games on the computer.

Her father, Keith, called her to come.

"Not now, Daddy," she said. "I'm working."

Randy's grown daughter's idea of a Father's Day present was obvious when she asked her mom, "Are we taking Daddy to the country club for lunch?"

Some dads get no respect.

Mary's husband, Gerald, is a well-educated science teacher and astronomer. So, naturally, when son Patrick wanted to know about black holes, she advised, "Go ask your father."

That's also why Patrick said, "I don't want to know *that* much about it."

Steve, 4, was so mad at his father that he hurled the worst insult he could think of: "Daddy, you're a Democracker!"

"Daddy," called out 5-year-old David.
His father peered down at him over the edge of the roof.
"Come down and tie my shoe."
Momma was standing right next to him.

Benjamin, 4, asked, "Mom, would you like a pet?"
"Well, no," Nan replied. "Would you?"
"Sure. We could have a dog or a cat or a goldfish.
Which would you like, Mom?"
"I would like a goldfish."
"Well, I would like a cat."
"Not a cat," Nan sighed. "Papa is allergic to cats."
"What's allergic?"
"It means that cats make him sneeze and feel miserable."
"Okay, Mom, I'll tell you what," Ben said thoughtfully.
"We'll get a cat, and Papa can move out."

The library of a Baptist church in Chapel Hill, North
Carolina featured live hamsters. Children loved to pay a visit to
Abrahamster and Sarah.
One Sunday morning, the teacher of the preschool
Sunday school class announced that she was going to bring in a
special guest. She began to give clues to describe Abrahamster.
"He's got hair all over, and he runs and runs and runs and then
he goes to sleep."
Aaron's hand shot up. The preacher's son shouted,
"My dad! My dad!"
His father, Mitch, has a beard.

Approaching his Big 4-0 birthday, Bill was sensitive
about looking his age. The Illinois father commented that he
needed to lose a few pounds.
His 8-year-old, Tyler, shook his head. "Dad, you're
slim, especially when you have on clothes."
Huh?

Theila, 5, and her mom, Carmen, were trying to get Dad's attention while he was watching TV.

After repeating themselves numerous times to no avail, Theila looked at Carmen, shaking her head. "You didn't know he was like this when you married him, did you?"

At about the age of 10, Harriet and her playmate Ginny sometimes got mad at each other. Their parents were friends, because both their fathers were lawyers in Worcester, Massachusetts.

In their spats, it was not unusual for one to taunt, "Your father's a liar; my father's a *lawyer!*"

Katherine overheard her friend's 5-year-old Alex ask, "Mom, what's a red-neck?"

Mom thought for a minute. "A red-neck is a rude, uncouth person."

"Oh," Alex said, as if he understood completely. "You mean like Daddy!"

DID *WHAT*?

Mothers and grandmothers like to tell what their children *said*. Fathers tell what their kids *did*.

John's family was living in student housing at Syracuse while he was a grad student. When he came home on an extremely hot summer afternoon, someone called to him that a Mr. Santini down the street wanted to talk with him.

Then he caught sight of his sons John, Jr., who was 4, and Bob, 3. He hadn't recognized them at first, but he instantly knew what had happened.

The complex's roads had just been resurfaced, and his boys were tarred head to toe.

All he could think of to take it off was gasoline. It took a considerable while, but he finally got around to asking, "Where's Mr. Santini?"

The guy lived a couple of blocks away, but as soon as John saw a certain car, he knew it was Santini's. On the trunk were small tar handprints. Over the roof, down the windshield and on the hood were little black footprints. On the side were fingerpainted waves of tar.

John 'fessed up that he was the culprits' father and offered to have Santini's car repainted. At the end of the conversation, John asked, "What kind of work are you in?"

Santini good-naturedly grinned. "I'm a Syracuse policeman."

In St. Albans, Vermont, Frank's two preschool-age sons went to visit a nearby neighbor friend and came back covered with white paint. Not fingerpaint, not even acrylic, but oil-based, lead-laden (turpentine scrubable) paint. The house next door was being painted.

Guess what color!

They start really early!

A new customer, Tim went into a bank with his wife, Dana, to open a checking account. He noticed that the banker, who had helped his wife and mother-in-law the day before, would not make eye contact. It really bothered him, and as soon as he and Dana left, he asked her, "What was *with* that guy?"

It took awhile for her to admit what had happened earlier. Their infant son. T. J. had been running his hand inside his well-endowed mother's shirt throughout the conversation.

Grandma had wise-cracked to the banker, "He's just like his father. He won't leave those things alone."

A Morristown, Tennessee, mom took her children to the nursery before going to work. Libby had been on the job for about an hour when Dad called.

"Are you missing anything?" he asked.

"No."

"Are you sure you haven't lost something?"

"No."

"Your purse?"

Her purse! She hadn't missed it. Neither had she seen her daughter Laura, 2, pitch it out of the back window of their car. Some guys at a gas station saw her do it, retrieved the purse and called Laura's father.

Robert, Jr., age 3, was playing on a jungle gym in their New York City neighborhood. His father was ready to go, but Junior didn't want to leave.

As Dad was reaching for him, little Robert kicked his Buster Brown shoes so hard in protest that he knocked out all of Dad's front teeth!

For Mother's Day, Robbie gave his wife Shirley and each of his four children a red carnation corsage to wear to church.

When Robin, 3, came out of Sunday school, her corsage was missing.

"What happened to your flower?" Shirley asked.

Robin grinned. "I ate it."

Bill was working on the roof of his Seneca, South Carolina home when he thought he heard Harriet, his wife, calling. Apparently, he didn't respond fast enough because she bellowed for all the neighbors to hear, "Get off the damn roof now! Chris has caught his penis in his zipper!"

He scrambled down to see his son howling in agony. Harriet had already tried to unzip Chris's shorts to no avail. Bill asked Harriet to get the scissors. "No!" wailed Chris, who was nursery-school age at the time.

Bill only wanted to cut the shorts off, but Chris imagined the worst. It didn't work anyway. The fabric would cut, but the metal zipper would not. Harriet hurried to call her daughter, Bonnie, to bring home the family car. Meanwhile, Bill was looking for his pliers.

"Are you crazy? Let's just go to the hospital!" shouted Harriet.

Chris had stopped crying by the time Bill and Bonnie got him to the emergency room. He was numb. Soon, the doctor was hard at work with his scalpel. Oops! He cut his...(Would you believe it?)...own finger. Bill handed over his pliers. That did the trick!

When they got home, Chris strutted in, displaying his new bandage. "Can I show this tomorrow at show-&-tell?"

While watching TV with his wife, Alan from Greensboro, North Carolina smelled something like perfume. He asked Meredith if it were hers. No. Perhaps they should investigate. It seemed to be coming from their 3-year-old's room. Mitchell was supposed to be asleep. Opening the door, they saw huge white clouds of baby powder.

Mitchell had been spraying the entire bottle, puff by puff, onto the ceiling fan, which had swished it around the room and into the closet, adhering it to the dark green walls, furniture and floor, even in the crevices (which became a year-long clean-up job).

"All I could see," said Alan, "were two brown eyes."

No matter what the age...

John was concerned about fire safety at the house he had bought for his family in upstate New York. His four boys had the two rooms upstairs in the wood frame home, so he bought a roll-up ladder.

He showed them how it attached at the window. "When you have a fire, break a window, if you have to, but pull the string and climb out of the house that way," he instructed briefly. "We'll have a fire drill soon."

John forgot about the promised drill until he came home to find a window broken in the one-story shed out back. Seeing the Jacob's ladder, he called his boys.

Sure enough, they had conducted their own drill.

Jim, a mild-mannered father, who never raised a hand to any of his children, was mortified when Junior developed an annoying habit. If Jim gave him a warning look whenever he misbehaved in church, Junior would cringe as though he was about to be hit.

Soon after their third child was born, Harriet and George were living and working in Augusta, Georgia, when the baby-sitter called Harriet in a panic. "I put Bonnie and Ricky in for their naps, and when I went upstairs, I found an empty bottle of baby aspirin. What should I do?"

George raced home to get the kids, who were 5 and 3. Harriet met them in the emergency room, sick with worry.

The doctor didn't pump their stomachs, because no one knew how much time had elapsed since they had consumed the bottle of aspirin, which had been full except for the one pill given to the baby. "Make them drink water to dilute the medication. Get as much into them as you can," he had told Harriet. "Check their breathing through the night, and if there's a problem, bring them in."

Both little bellies were so distended from all that water, Harriet and George were afraid they would explode. Harriet sat up all night, making sure they were breathing, terrified that they might die.

The next day, both seemed to be fine. Bonnie awoke first. "That Ricky is so selfish!" she said. "He only gave me one."

Billy and Michelle were having a conversation before bedtime. They heard a muffled noise.

"Do you think the kids are up?" Michelle wondered aloud.

Billy listened and couldn't hear a sound from their three children. "No, I don't think so."

Just then, the cat scampered into the room wearing little Grace's bathrobe.

While introducing his boys to the adventure of fishing in South Florida, Mike amazed them with stories of growing up near Lake Worth. They wanted to know more.

"Did you catch any sharks in Lake Worth, Daddy?"

"Or giant squids?"

Mike changed the subject pronto and baited a hook.

Soon, Gabe, 6, cried out, "Daddy, I've got something!"

Sure enough he had hooked a 30-pounder—his little brother.

They really get active when you have guests!

Arch's boss, a multi-millionaire who owned the state's third largest car dealership, was visiting Arch at home on behalf of their church.

38

Arch and his wife Janet were telling him good-bye on the front porch when the boss began to laugh. Their son, Rob, 3, was peeing off the porch.

After the boss was gone, Janet turned to her husband. "Arch, I'm so embarrassed. He will think Rob has no home training."

Arch wasn't upset at all. He recalled an incident when a woman screamed in the dealership's lot. People ran to see what was the matter. The owner and his brother were both peeing in the parking lot.

While entertaining friends at their home in La Grange, Georgia, John and Linda were presiding at the dinner table when their 3-year-old daughter Emily danced in. She was wearing her pink mesh tutu—and nothing more!

Peter's parents were hosting a dinner party to entertain Dad's bosses from work. Peter, 6, was sent to play out back.

He decided to play gas station: took out the garden hose and filled up all the parked cars with "gas."

It's not always just YOUR kids!

Darrell and his wife, Gail, hit upon a great idea to earn extra baby-sitting co-op "tokens." They would baby-sit with several other couples' children on New Year's Eve in separate locations in their town of Lynchburg, Virginia.

Darrell ended up with five munchkins, ranging in age from 2 to 9 (none his own) at somebody else's house. About bedtime, one little girl punched her brother hard enough to draw blood, lots of it. Darrell rushed them into the bathroom to wash off the telltale signs of battle and patch him up. Meanwhile, the other three, none of whom lived in that home, found red poster paint and made a lovely stripe from one end of the living room carpet to the other.

Darrell's advice to dads: never let kids outnumber you.

Some kids tell on themselves!

The next door neighbors at their duplex had just bought a new stationwagon, a shiny silver color. Johnny, 10, thought it would be prettier yellow. He found some paint in their garage and painted it for them.

"Did Dad have to pay for a new paint job?" I asked Johnny, now grown.

"Nope. New car. Something about paint in the gas tank."

DAD SAID *WHAT*? DID *WHAT*?

Sometimes, what Papa says is more fascinating than kids' comments.

Branko, who works in McLean, Virginia, was telling me about his son, Alex, who came running in with a paper and a crayon saying, "What's our credit card number? There's some really cool stuff on TV, and the man says all you need is a credit card."

"How old is Alex?" I asked.

Branko thought a moment. "Six. Older than that, they *know* the credit card number."

Our long-awaited newly-adopted child, Joy, stood at a footstool in our den, looking at her favorite picture book. She touched her finger to the cat on the cover and said, "Kit-ty."

"Did you hear that? Did you hear that?" my husband Randy exclaimed, jumping from his chair. "She said 'Daddy!'"

Franco, an Italian immigrant in New York, overheard his children arguing about the Statue of Liberty. His daughters were sure she was a female. Dominic, his son, insisted the statue was a man. Franco knew who to call for an answer.

"Hello," he said. "Is the Statue of Liberty a lady or a man?"

He had dialed Information.

Sometimes, Granddad says something odd.

Anna's grandfather was surprised when the 3-year-old, modeling new silky swimwear, swished around and stuck out her bottom. "Feel my bathing suit," she said, beaming.

"Not on your life," said Paul to a small audience. "I wouldn't go to jail for anyone!"

Granddad is a police officer.

Sometimes Dad gets quoted.

While shoe shopping with her son, Mary Lisi from Monroe, Connecticut, was trying to decide whether to buy the $80 ones. "That seems a little steep," she told the salesperson.

Wavering back and forth, she was wondering, should she? Or shouldn't she?

"Mom, you know what Dad would say," said Sam, who was 6. "You're a money pit like the dog."

These fathers did WHAT?

Zipping along I-95 on a trip from New York to Washington, Jarvis was approaching the Baltimore Tunnel when Tiffany, who had been snoozing in the back seat of his Mercedes awoke.

"Where's Ashley?" she asked, looking for her twin.

Her 8-year-old brother was asleep in the front seat, but Ashley, who had been sleeping next to her, was gone.

Jarvis admitted he "went crazy." Panicky, he notified the Maryland State Police, suspecting that she had been kidnapped. Near the Delaware Memorial Bridge on the New Jersey Turnpike two hours earlier, he had stopped at a rest area to use the facilities, leaving his children napping in the car.

A computer-check later, Ashley was found safe in New Jersey at a state police station near the rest stop where she, too, had used the bathroom.

After telling a gas station attendant that her father had left her, Ashley was taken to the Moorestown barracks, where she played on a computer, toured the station, was photographed in a holding cell and ate all the ice cream and sodas she wanted.

Daddy ate crow.

Ted termed their cookout "salvaging the evening." He had invited Charlie and his two children over for supper with him and his two little ones, while the wives had a night out.

Four kids to two caretakers is better than a day care center ratio, but these guys were enjoying themselves that winter night, and suddenly they realized that their two-year-olds were missing. They called out "Lindsay!" "Little Charlie!"

Usually, when Lindsay would hide, she'd be giggling within in a minute or two. This time, no giggles. Ted and Charlie hunted all over the house and then out in the yard, calling all the while. No response.

After about 30 minutes, they wisely phoned for help. Six police officers joined the search. Curious neighbors gawked. Although they spread out for about 15 minutes, the police insisted that they search the house again. Ted told them that he and Charlie had already looked everywhere inside.

On his first sweep, an officer found them both in a bedroom, asleep under the rolled back covers at the foot of the bed.

Ted sheepishly defended himself. "We looked *under* the bed."

Thomas stopped by a friend's home briefly and spoke with his friend's mother, Elise. "I'm in a hurry," said Thomas. "Tommy's in the car."

"You should never leave a child alone in a car," cautioned Elise.

"Oh, he's all right. Look," said Thomas turning toward the old Chrysler with the push-button gears.

They looked—and watched the car roll down a hill and crash into a tree.

As a counselor for Troop 33, Bryan's dad, Dean, was leading a group of boys up a mountain near Saranac Lake, New York.

They paused at a beautiful stream when Dean said, "C'mon guys, let's get a drink."

They did. But just around the bend upstream, they felt

sickish when they saw two dirty dogs lying in the water.

The climb was tough on an uncertain trail. Half the troop turned back. The rest, led by Dean, struggled up to a lookout point. Once there, filthy and bedraggled, they met other people who were clean and barely winded. How could that be?

They had come up a different trail. The one Dean had led them up had been condemned ten years ago.

Ralph had just scolded Hannah for putting hot coffee into a plastic cup. He had explained why: the cup would melt.

Then he inadvertently placed the filled cup on the stove's burner.

Lesson learned.

Eating her salad before dinner, Jordan's daughter, Lindsey, was a bit messy. Jordan picked up a piece of cauliflower from the table and popped it into his mouth. It tasted weird.

Lindsey watched him curiously. "Dad, why are you eating my Pla-Doh?"

Bill's stepdaughter, Candy, 7, came home from school all upset. Several of her friends were wearing casts. Others were signing and drawing pictures on them. "I wish I had one," she said wistfully.

"You don't have to break a bone," said Bill, who adored her. "I'll make you one."

The next afternoon, Candy came in, happily showing off all the notes and drawings on her arm's new cast.

Their 2-year-old son, Hokey, was running to jump on his bed when he hit his head on the bookcase headboard. His parents had to take him to the hospital.

Nurses wouldn't let Coralee go into the examining room with her son because she was pregnant, explaining that the trauma might be disturbing to mother and unborn son. Coralee insisted anyway.

The bloody scene did move her to tears, and macho-man Herman patted his wife on the shoulder. "Now Hon," he said, "you'll have to get used to this. You'll be here a lot. Boys are like this, always getting hurt." With that, Herman fainted.

Soon, he was on a stretcher next to Hokey.

When Bet was a little girl, the family used to talk about "poor tired Daddy," referring to Ernest, her father.

They often repeated a story he had told on himself: he was so tired one night that he came home, climbed the stairs, ripped off his shirt, threw it in the toilet and pitched his gum in the laundry hamper.

Only when Bet grew older did she reassess that tale. "Daddy was a dentist. He never chewed gum in his life," she told me. "Think about it!"

(What REALLY went into that hamper?)

Jean, a mother from Baltimore, had to be at church early on Easter Sunday, so she asked her husband, Mike, to help the girls dress and bring them in time for the children's parade. Libby, 5, and Kitty, 3, were both in the procession.

And so, during the service, Mom turned around to see her girls proudly parading down the aisle in their pretty new slips.

CRIME & PUNISHMENT, KID STYLE

So who has never been more naughty than nice? Put yourself in *their* shoes.

"Daddy told a lie!" tattled Jonathan, 3, to his father's parents, who live in the Chicago area.

True, very true. Brian had told a bill collector he wasn't home. And what was his parents' reaction? They grounded him! And required him to do chores, like mow their lawn. Furthermore, he had to write a letter to his son apologizing for lying.

And how did the grounding part work, since they were not living in the same house?

Brian's wife saw to it that he got to bed early.

An antique car buff, Paul had just bought a '69 Cougar and had not yet gotten a license tag. Nevertheless, he offered to take his twin daughters to the corner store to get some gum.

Her sister was ready to go, but Capri balked. "I'm not going to the store with you. You might get arrested and go to jail, and I'm not going to jail."

A few minutes later, Capri was headed to the car with the others. Paul questioned her change of heart.

"Oh, well," she said, "if you go to jail, I'll go with you. We'll have fun!"

It's important to follow through.

Matt, 9, and Ryan, 5, had been threatened with military school if they didn't "shape up." Mom and Dad kept a tally of demerits on the refrigerator. Both boys had been especially bad during the Christmas holidays.

One morning, Dad announced that they were going to take a long ride. He was very secretive about where the family was headed.

After many miles, their car pulled into a large parking lot near some high fences.

Matt refused to get out of the car.

"Please, please, I'll be good!" Ryan cried. "Give me one more chance! I don't want to go to military school!"

His brother's tension eased. "It's okay, we can get out," Matt soothed. He had seen the sign and knew that SPCA meant they had come to get a dog.

The real question is: did they learn something?

Floyd Junior knew that the front closet door was never locked. But right before Christmas it was.

"Why is this damn door locked?" he demanded to know.

His mother immediately punished him. He was screaming when Floyd came home from work.

"What's wrong?" Floyd asked.

Still crying, his son blubbered, "Mama washed out my mouth with that damn soap."

Brent Junior's mother, Vickie, is a housewife; Brent, his dad, owns a construction company.

Brent was quite young but talking well, when Vickie punished him for disobedience, sending him to his room and bed.

Checking on him later, she said, "Well, son, I hope you know now that when Mommy tells you to do something you must do it."

"Are you my boss?" he asked.

"Yes, I guess you could say that."

Brent Junior thought a moment, head cocked. "Mommy, is Daddy a woman?"

Another question: who punishes whom?

Jean was spanking her son, James, when he began howling, "No! Daddy's s'posed to do that!"

Brandon from Reading, Pennsylvania, wondered aloud, "Can you imagine how big the naughty chair would be for God?"

BIRDS, BEES, ADULT TREES
& ANATOMIES

Why is it so hard to explain sex and anatomy to our own children? Why if it weren't for....

Jackie's parents were listening to him recite the Ten Commandments. They stopped him at the seventh. "Do you know what that means?"

"Sure," he replied proudly. "Don't cut adult trees."

No one corrected him.

When their children were 10 and 11, Alice and Lucas decided it was time to explain the facts of life. Well-rehearsed, Alice took their daughter, Lisa, into one room and Lucas talked with son Bucky in another. Lesson over, they compared notes.

Lisa had been indignant. "I'm never going to do *that!*"

Bucky was aghast. "You mean you did that *twice?*"

At about age 10, Richie came in telling his mother some things he'd heard about sex. He asked her to tell him more. "I think you ought to talk with your Daddy," Annelle said.

After a brief discussion with his father Dick, Richie returned. "*You'd* better tell me. He doesn't know any more than I do. He said, 'Tell me what you already know.'"

This topic brings out some interesting questions.

Kenny grinned while the bride and groom were kissing. People in the pews heard him ask his parents in a loud whisper. "Has he sprinkled the pollen on her yet?"

Ralph and Beth from Parma, Ohio, were quietly eating breakfast, when their 3-year-old son, Jason, spied the extra "vitamin" next to Beth's plate.

Beth explained that the medicine was going to "help Mommy have another baby."

After mulling this over, Jason turned to his father. "Mommy needs the medicine to get me a baby brother or sister, right Daddy?"

Ralph nodded.

"If *you* take one, would we have a dog?"

So pleased that Bart would soon marry his mother, Buddy wanted to know if he could call Bart "Dad."

He was also curious about what came next and asked, "Mom, when you and Dad get married, are you going to do the 'S' word?"

While playing dolls, Katy from Grand Rapids, Michigan, looked up and asked her father, "Do you think I'll ever get married?"

"That's up to you, Katy," said Andy.

"Will I marry a boy?"

"I hope so."

She smoothed out her doll's hair. "Gee, I wonder what I'll name him."

Birds, Bees and Babies

Lee's friend Beth was expecting. Lee's 2-year-old was curious about the whole thing.

Sarah was told that the daddy, Mike, had put the baby into Beth's stomach.

Later, Sarah was patting her own round stomach. "I have a baby in my tummy," she announced.

Now Lee was the curious one. "How did it get there?"

"Daddy put it there."

In Roanoke, Virginia, Stephanie, 3, came downstairs and slid into her place for breakfast. "I've got a baby in my tummy," she announced.

"You do?" said Terry, calmly, putting down his coffee mug. "How do you know?"

"'Cause I heard him growling."

Robin had a riddle for his children, Mallory, 9, Megan, 6, and Ben, 4. "Who is short, can't walk, can't talk, sometimes stinks and is coming to live with us in February?"

"A drunk man," they decided.

The answer, of course, was a sibling. To which Mallory replied, "A baby?! Where are we going to get a baby?"

Okay, Robin, explain that riddle! Your kids may not *want* a drunk man in February.

Sarasota residents Robert and Barbara waited until Robert's birthday to tell their three children, ages 14, 12 and 10, that they were going to have an addition to the family.

Their youngest was stunned by the news. "I didn't know you could do that. I thought you were too old!"

While watching Tunk shave, Tunky, 5, mused, "When little boys grow up, they're daddies, aren't they?" Getting a nod, he continued, "And little girls grow up to be mommies."

"Yes, and anything else you want to know," said Tunk, "ask your mother."

Alan believed in telling it all and using biological terms with his children. And so when his son, Darryl, asked, "Where did I come from?" Alan matter-of-factly explained the facts of life.

Darryl, who was 5, seemed pleased to know all this new information. He looked up at Alan. "Can I watch next time?"

Certain body parts take some explanation, too.

"Boys have penises," announced Henry, 4, to his dad, Loyd. Just then, Henry's mother walked by in her bathrobe. He nodded to Loyd. "And girls have pajamas."

While his twin sons were taking a bath, Ed was eavesdropping and heard the following discussion:
Charlie: "I have a 'peanut,' so I'm a boy."
Alex: "I have a peanut, too, so I'm a boy. But what does Sister have?"
Charlie: "Peanut butter."

Erica, 4, from Safety Harbor, Florida, was waving her clasped hands back and forth below her waist. "Mommy," she said. "I want one of those things like Daddy has."

Grandfather Griff was walking with granddaughter Alex, 33 months, behind her golden retrievers. "Where's your tail, Alex?" he teased.
"Grumps, don't you know I don't have a tail," she said impatiently. "I have a vagina."

An Episcopal priest in Alexandria, Neal had enrolled his son Cliff at an Episcopal diocesan school.
When Cliff was in the fourth grade, Neal and his wife Carol got a call from the family life (sex education) teacher.
On the day they discussed the difference between male and female anatomy, Cliff was paying very close attention. When the teacher mentioned a female body part that sounded familiar to Cliff, he raised his hand and proclaimed, "My mom has a blue one now. She used to have a white one."
At first she was shocked, then she realized he was referring to his mom's automobile, a Volvo, instead of a similar sounding body part.

SOMEBODY CONTROL THIS CHILD!

Why is it that your child will say or do something in public that you simply can't predict —or control?

While Mike and his mother Pam were grocery shopping with his son, little Neil told of an "urgent" need. Mike took Neil by the hand to the bathroom.

Soon Neil came running back down the aisle shouting, "Grammy! Grammy! Daddy peed in the sink."

Mike shrunk down with embarrassment.

Neil had never seen a urinal before.

At a Chinese restaurant in Tewksbury, Massachusetts, Daddy Dana was surprised when Jessica, 4, spoke to some middle-aged strangers nearby.

"We have two dogs, Alex and Cracker," she said. "Guess what! Alex does poop-poop on the sofa."

Exhibitors at a gun show, Skip and his wife Becky from Kansas were each talking to someone but saw that the customers' eyes were looking beyond them.

Skip turned around to see their daughter Jessica in the back of the booth breast-feeding her Cabbage Patch doll.

Five-year-old Laurie and her little brother accompanied their parents to Raleigh to buy a new home. Her father, Frank, had been transferred by a company that was shutting down its Charlotte office. The family had found a suitable house, paid a down payment and signed the papers.

En route home, Laurie's folks changed their minds.

They pulled off the highway to phone the realtor and say that they were stopping payment on the check. Frank would resign from the company on Monday morning, but they would attend the Saturday party to bid farewell to everyone, who would soon scatter across the map.

The party, a picnic for all the departing families, was hosted by the boss. His wife asked Laurie how she liked her new room in the Raleigh house.

To her parents' still-felt embarrassment and the shock of those standing nearby, Laurie chirped, "We're not moving to Raleigh!"

Ahmed was attending a convention where he was to receive an award. His son Tareq accompanied him.

A prestigious colleague was giving a speech to a packed room. She faltered, and suddenly the words were no longer coming out. Just "uhs."

Tareq grew impatient. In his loudest voice (of course), he said what the adults were probably thinking. "Yeah? What?"

In Morgan County, Kentucky, population about 2,000, there are virtually no ethnic minorities. Not many shopping centers, either. So Dad took his son Wesley, 3, shopping in neighboring Round County.

Wesley was inspecting some toys when he looked up and saw an African-American gentleman. "Look, Dad!" he said, pointing. "It's Hammer Man!"

Mike, a deejay for a 100,000-watt Tampa radio station couldn't find a babysitter. He had to take Jimmy, 4, to work with him.

While Mike was doing his show, Jimmy was playing behind his chair.

Suddenly, Mike was off the air, and no amount of button-pushing could get him back on. Jimmy, you see, had fiddled with a switch and cut off the transmitter.

Why is it that so many of those embarrassing experiences happen at church?

It can start really early. A Presbyterian minister was holding Rebecca, not more than 6 months, to baptise her. He was talking too much, so she put a "shut up" hand on his mouth. With difficulty, he continued and then handed her back to Jeff, her father.

Turning to the congregation, he asked, "Ever tried to talk with a finger up your nose?"

Greg, a minister in Rock Hill, South Carolina, was preaching when his daughter got away from his wife and ran up to the pulpit. In a voice which carried to the back pew, she said, "Daddy, Daddy, I go tee-tee all by myself!"

Three-year-old Scott was misbehaving during the Presbyterian worship service. His father picked him up, threw him over his shoulder and strode up the aisle to the door.

Wide-eyed Scott looked back at the congregation. "Pray for me!"

Mark was oblivious while his son, Trevor, 4, was crawling under pews and rolling on the floor of their Moravian church. Horrified, Melissa, in the choir, began pointing and making faces to get Mark to take control of their boy.

The only one who didn't notice was Mark. And the talk of the church became: "What's wrong with Melissa?"

It's Easter Sunday at a Charlotte church with a preacher known for his long-windedness. At the stroke of noon, an alarm sounds: Brrriiinnngggg!

The "brrrriiinnnggging" continues while David, 7, reaches for the travel alarm in his pocket. Dad beats him to it. But Walt's hand is too big for that little pocket.

Finally, David wins out. But to turn it off, he must open it up. BRRRIIINNNGGG!

By then, the congregation is beyond reverence, practically rolling on the floor.

The visiting evangelist at a small mountain church droned on and on. At 12:40 p.m. he was showing no signs of wrapping up the sermon.

Before her mother could react, the preacher's daughter stood up on the pew, turned to the congregation and said, "Does anybody here know how to stop this guy?"

They really get cranked up at weddings.

Before Bart and Theresa of Florence, South Carolina, were married, they used to take Theresa's son Buddy along on their dates. With his prospective step-son Buddy, 9, in the back seat, Bart would give Theresa a quick good-night kiss.

"I saw that!" Buddy would always say.

"Good," Bart would say. "Watch again." And he would give her another.

At their wedding, after the nuptial kiss, Buddy yelled from the congregation, "I saw that!"

"Good. Watch again."

Their son, the ring bearer, got hot. He left the stage during the upstate New York ceremony and disappeared.

Mom and Dad didn't know whether to chase after him or discreetly leave.

But a couple of minutes later, he reappeared—totally undressed—and stepped back into his place on stage.

The groom's 2-year-old son, Will, was sitting on the front row. At a most inopportune time, he stood to yell, "Ride 'em cowboy!"

61

People frowned until he turned around to announce to all who might not know, "My daddy's a saddle bronc rider!"

Pennies had been placed on the church floor to mark where each person in the wedding should stand. Ralph's son Teddy, the ring bearer, couldn't resist. Halfway through the service, he handed the pillow to Ralph, an usher, and crawled around picking up pennies.

Ralph was the only one not enjoying the show, especially when an uncle spoke up from his pew, "Raise the kid's allowance!"

Their son, Chris was the ring bearer. Nan and Bud were also in the wedding party. Suddenly, after they had reached the chancel, Chris disappeared. Nan saw him peek from behind the minister's robe. She couldn't reach him. He ignored her.

The robe began to rise. Then Chris was on the floor peering up to see what was under it. He changed positions for a better view. Feet in the air, he appeared on the other side looking up the robe. The minister never missed a word.

But Bud had seen enough. He left his place and strode toward his son. By that time, Chris was crouched, feet on the floor, head down, still gazing at the clergyman's legs. Bud snatched his son's belt and carried him in the same bent position out a side door. Chris never howled, just grinned like a Cheshire cat.

Later, the minister admitted that, because it was such hot day, he had worn only underwear beneath his heavy black robe.

MULTIPLE KIDS NEED
MULTIPLE PARENTS

How do they do it? People who have their children one at a time wonder how a mother can take care of two or more the same age. But dads have similar stresses. They need to have a sense of humor, too.

Sue and Joe of Apex, North Carolina brought their triplets home with much ado.

After the excitement came the sleepless nights and some semblance of routine with Matthew, Cody and Chelsea.

A few weeks later, Joe offered to do night duty. That evening, he slept on the floor of the babies' room.

"He was afraid he wouldn't hear them," Sue laughed. "Three babies, and he didn't think he'd hear them!"

As the triplets grew, Joe would rush through dinner after work so he could play with them.

One night, he put gel in their hair to make "teenage music idols."

Another night, Joe said, "Look, Sue."

His wife looked over to see all three babies in an L.L. Bean bag.

"A Bean bag of babies!"

When their triplets were small, they worked together to drive Joe and Sue crazy.

The safety-conscious parents purchased cabinet locks by the dozens and would have to put three on each cabinet. No problem for Matthew, Cody and Chelsea. One would pull open the door. One would push down on the lock. One would pull

out all the stuff. All at one time.

To reach things, two would lie on the floor and the other one would stand on the two to get whatever they wanted.

Sue had been concentrating very hard on potty training their 3-year-old triplets. She had tried handing out M&Ms for remaining on the pot at group potty sittings.

At the time, she and Joe were living in a very small apartment, with no washer or dryer.

Joe woke up one morning and announced, "No poopy diapers are allowed in the new house."

The next day, they were all three potty trained.

Sue asks, "How did he do that?"

Scott was babysitting with their 2-year-old triplets during naptime. Annette had been having trouble getting them to go to sleep, but every time Scott, who was working in the garage, stuck his head in the door, all was quiet.

As Annette said later, "When they are quiet, I know they are busy."

The fourth time he checked, about an hour after Annette had left, he heard a giggle and ran upstairs.

One had pooped in her pull-ups, so they had taken it to flush. While there, Brittany and Courtney had unraveled all the toilet paper and strewn it around. With the scoop Annette used to wash their hair, they had dipped up potty water and splashed it everywhere. One had gotten into the cabinet and found the shampoo, lotion and bubble bath.

The "clean freak," Abby, never got out of her bed. She just squirted the shampoo, lotion and bubble bath her sisters had brought in all over her covers and the room.

When Annette arrived and saw the mess, Scott was defensive: "Why didn't you lock the bathroom before you left?"

During a children's song at their Lutheran Church, twin boys, Mark and Christopher, 3, started flipping up the girls' dresses. Tony, the pastor, gave their mother, Christina, "the look." As soon as Christina stood up, the boys scattered. So she began chasing them through the sanctuary. She finally caught both of them in a football hold.

"I made the mistake of putting one down to close the door," said Christina, "and Mark ran back into the church."

She was in tears by that time, so a friend brought Mark back to her.

"I deposited the twins in the nursery and left," she said. "The nursery workers knew when I had had enough."

Tony was upset and embarrassed, too. He's the twins' dad.

Tony, a Sumter, South Carolina, dad, and a golfing friend were putting on the eighth green when the golf cart began moving. Tony's 22-month-old twins were operating it.

Mark and Christopher had been intently watching to see how it worked and decided to give it a try. One was steering while the other pushed the gas pedal, driving it right into the nearby pond.

Tony and his friend took off after it. When it hit the pond, Christopher fell out and the cart pinned his leg. With one hand, Tony picked up the cart and scooped Christopher up with the other. Golfers came running from all over the course. The cart was stuck in the mud and could not be pushed out. Word quickly got around, and the golf pro was soon on hand with chains to pull it out.

No one ever asked Tony how come he took 22-month-old twins golfing. It's a "guy thing," huh?

Soon after moving his family to Germany, George took his twin daughters, 3, to visit a nearby palace. As they were walking around the palace grounds, Allison and Andrea suddenly disappeared.

A father's panic turned into embarrassment as he noticed a trail of clothes. Shoes, then socks, then shirts, shorts, underpanties—all leading to a marble fountain.

There, before 100 onlookers, were his birth-day naked girls, laughing and splashing, having a better time than anyone else.

George from Lynchburg, Virginia, recalls the day he learned that identical twins don't necessarily have identical personalities.

He arrived home from the office and walked by his 5-year-old daughters' room. Hearing music from Andrea's cassette player, he knocked and entered for a visit. Andrea was lying on her bed with tears streaming down her cheeks.

"What's wrong, Honey?" George asked.

"Daddy, 'Swan Lake' is so beautiful; it just makes me cry when I listen to it."

His other daughter, Allison, was at her desk intently working on some small project. She laughed, "But it's great music to work to!"

"What are you doing over there, Allison?"

"Picking legs off ants!"

"We got really tired of people asking, 'Are they all yours?'" said Jeff, the father of quads Caroline, Joshua, James and Adam.

He told of a day at the mall, when his children were a year old. His wife, Miriam, was pushing one double stroller; his sister-in-law, the other.

After the third or fourth stranger had asked, "Are they all yours?" Jeff responded, "Yes, they're mine, but two are hers." He pointed to his wife. "And two are hers," he said pointing to his sister-in-law.

No more comments.

TEENS—TOO TRYING FOR WORDS

If you thought the "terrible twos" were tough, you'll wish you could return to *those* blissful years, when your kids turn teen. At least, in earlier days, you had some degree of control and credibility.

"What's it like having four teenagers all the same age?" I asked quad dad Jeff.

"Well, they're 15, and they think they know it all," he said. "That makes us four times as dumb."

What do fathers worry most about? Their teens driving? Doing drugs?

Elizabeth's driving record was an embarrassment to both her parents. As she was leaving to return to college, her father sternly warned her not to get another speeding ticket. A few hours later, the phone rang, and her mother answered. "Elizabeth wants to talk to you," she said, calling to her husband in another room.

Thomas was seething as soon as he heard her say, "I got stopped by the highway patrol." She quickly added, "Dad, the patrolman found some marijuana in the back seat."

His demeanor switched from anger to horror. "No, Elizabeth, no!" Horrible thoughts brought sobs. Where had he gone wrong? How long had this been going on? Was she addicted? What would his fellow state legislators, or his constituents, think? He had advocated getting tough on drugs. How could he deal with her—or them?

He was still emotional when she said, "Just kidding, Dad. I only got a speeding ticket."

His relief was evident. "Is that all? Are you sure? Don't worry, I'll get a lawyer to help you."

He wasn't even mad at Elizabeth's mother, Jane, who had suggested the ploy to show him how all things are relative.

Both parents were called by school personnel to come immediately. Their daughter Janine had been overheard telling friends she was running away from home. The caller didn't know details, but they had detained her in the principal's office.

Melanie and Ralph raced to the high school from their offices and met in the parking lot. Janine had just gotten her driver's license, and her grandfather had given her his old car. There sat the Chevy nearby—full of teenage odds and ends.

"She must be serious," said Ralph visibly shaken. "There's Pokey."

Pokey was the tiny teddy bear she still slept with.

Her parents were reluctant to let Babs borrow the car because it was the only one the family owned. Generally, Babs was a responsible child, but she had just gotten her license. So they set some limits.

Babs could drive her best friend (but no one else) to the Sunday night youth meeting at church (but nowhere else) and must be home before dark (it was daylight savings time).

As the best friend, I can attest that she drove carefully to the church. But her boyfriend, Dan, wasn't there. In fact, Dan had been seen with a girl named Ann at school that week. As we were turning toward home, Babs thought aloud, "I bet I know where Dan is."

With that, she headed in the opposite direction. I knew we were both in trouble when she entered another neighborhood far from home.

Sure enough, there was Dan's car. And there was Dan, seated on a sofa in front of a picture window, his arm around Ann. "Doesn't bother me a bit," she said haughtily, as she drove completely up a guy wire on the telephone pole across the street.

The front tires were still spinning as we jumped down from our perch. Dan and Ann came running out to see what

idiot had hit the pole. "Babs! What are *you* doing here?" he said. Ann ran back to her house.

Babs was too hysterical and too scared to call her parents. Her dad would be furious; her mom, devastated. That was the family's only car. Besides, someone else would have to drive us home, because only a wrecker could take that car anywhere.

I reluctantly called my father to explain the predicament and ask him to come. Then *I* became the furious one. Daddy was laughing himself silly.

Their drinking?

Joe and Mary arrived home after an overnight summer visit and were relieved to find the house still standing. Despite their admonitions to their two teenagers not to have any parties, they wondered if the temptation of no chaperones would be too great.

They checked the house carefully. It had been freshly vacuumed. Mary peered into the garbage. No beer cans. Later, Joe was walking in the backyard and spied the remains of a block of ice. He smugly called John, his oldest, for an explanation.

Without blinking, John retorted, "We had the biggest freak hailstorm you ever saw last night."

Steve, at 16, had been grounded by Fred for drinking and coming in late. To Steve, his life was over. A particular party was too important to miss. He begged and pleaded with Fred. Finally a deal was struck: he could go, but no drinking and be home on time at 11 p.m.

Fred's blood pressure went up as minutes ticked closer to "pumpkin hour." Five, four, three, two... He heard a shuffling at the back door. Fred opened it.

There stood a very drunk Steve pointing clown-like to his watch. "On time!"

Their dates?

No one in the family liked Chappie's new boyfriend. He was nothing like Spike, their favorite. Dad had tried to express his displeasure, but she didn't care. One day, the guy parked his truck in front of Grandmother's house to visit Chappie there. Standing outside, Grandmother eyed him and said, "No one with dirty fingernails will come into *my* house!"

End of boyfriend. He drove away into oblivion.

Chuck's daughter Tina, 13, was excited about her new boyfriend. "He's Italian!" she told her dad with glee.

The Cary, North Carolina teen was even more elated when he invited her to his home. "We're going to have an Italian dinner!" she gushed. "I just *love* Italian food."

The next night at the supper table, Chuck asked Tina how the evening went.

"Oh, it was wonderful! His mother cooks the best Italian food," she said.

"What did you have?"

"Polish sausage!"

Or what you DON'T know?

All grown up, Garret was reminiscing with Aldo, his dad, about his teen years in New Jersey. "One of my greatest memories about being 15 was coming in after mowing the lawn and being able to get a beer afterwards.

Aldo: "You WHAT?!"

At 25, Edward from Hickory, North Carolina was having a drink with his father Bob, talking about his crazy teenage years. "When I'm 30," he said, "I'll tell you all the things I did in high school that you didn't know about."

"Well, before you do," said Bob, taking another gulp, "I'll tell you all the things you thought you got away with."

You've probably seen the "Simple Rules for Dating My Daughter" on the Internet if you now have a teenage daughter. It's too long to quote entirely, but here are the highlights, sent to me by my friend Jordan from Boston. You may want to add a few more.

"If you honk from the driveway, you'd better be delivering a parcel, because you are not picking anything—or anyone—up.

"You may not touch my daughter in front of me or peer at anything below her neck. If you cannot keep your hands or eyes off of her, I will remove them.

"If you must follow the trendy fashion of wearing huge droopy pants with your underwear showing, I will not object. But to assure that your clothes do not fall off during your date with my daughter, I will fasten them securely to your waist with my electric nail gun.

"Forget the small talk. Just tell me when you will have her safely home. Use the word 'early.'

"No matter how popular you are, you will date no one but my little girl until she is finished with you. If you make her cry, I will make you cry.

"Inappropriate places for a date: places where there are no parents, policemen or nuns within eyesight; places which have beds, sofas, darkness or enough heat to induce her to wear shorts or other skimpy attire. Romantic movies with sexual themes should be avoided; violent ones are okay. Hockey games are fine; old folks homes are preferable.

"If I ask where you are going and with whom, you have one chance to tell the truth and nothing but the truth. Do not lie to—or trifle with—me.

"Be afraid. I just might mistake the sound of your car for a chopper coming in over a rice paddy near Hanoi. As soon as you pull in the driveway, exit your car with both hands in plain view. Speak the perimeter password, announce that you two have arrived safely and early, deliver her to the door and then return to your car without entering the house. The camouflaged face in the window is mine!"

RIDICULOUS ROLE REVERSAL

When does it happen? The father becomes the child; the child, the parent. Too soon.

In a large hardware store in Greensboro, North Carolina, Mike was looking at the display of power tools. "I really need this," he said, holding up a hand drill.

"Daddy," chided Ellison, 3, "that's not a *need*. That's a *want*."

"I'm going to the bicycle store. Come with me," Brett said to his 5-year-old son, Foard.

"I don't want to," said Foard.

"Come on. It won't take long."

"No."

"Son, let's go," Brett urged one more time.

Foard was adamant. "Just be a man, Dad! Go on by yourself."

David from Hillsborough, New Jersey, was reprimanding his son Alex, who was not much over 2.

Alex frowned and shook his finger at his father. "You go to work!"

At our church's Sunday worship service, we were seated next to a family I did not recognize: a father, his son, about 13, and a daughter, around 10. When they passed the friendship pad, I heard some snickering, mostly from Dad.

My first thought when the pad passed to my hands was, "Don't they know they are supposed to put last names?" In a childlike scrawl was "Adam, Rachel and Big A."

When the service was over, I turned to Dad and said, "Well, I suppose you're 'Big A.'"

"No, he is," he replied, pointing to his son.

"Then who does that make you?" I asked, anticipating "A the Great" or "Bigger A."

"Big A's father."

When asked whether their family had experienced role reversal, Jim didn't have to ponder a moment. "My daughters have been telling me where to go for years."

Interesting. Jim has two daughters—and one son!

Sometimes the reversal goes the other way.

Like most kids, Matt from Duluth, Georgia, just had to have that cereal that had been so heavily-advertised on all the TV kiddie shows. He got his way, and the next day was crunching his first bite from the cherished box.

He chewed and chomped, finally swallowing. "This stuff tastes like dog food!" he cried in a most un-Mikey manner.

Mom and Dad were snickering. "It is."

Even when everyone is older....

Remember how you hated it when your parents arranged a date for you? Now, children and even grandchildren have assumed that role.

Tom's daughter, Robin, was arranging a blind date for him. She was trying to describe to the woman his attractive appearance.

Kala, his granddaughter, spoke up, "Yeah, he's cute for an old man."

Of course, that description got back to him—over and over.

Their three adult children announced that, for their anniversary, Robbye and Harold were invited to enjoy a wonderful dinner at the home of one of their daughters.

The threesome began by offering valet service when Mom and Dad drove up. At the front door, one of them was handing out glasses of champagne. Flowers were on the table. Another announced that, in just a moment, they would be served a "wonderful dinner." And then they brought out fish sticks, frozen french fries and green Jell-o gelatin.

They recognized the menu immediately. Every Friday night, when a baby sitter would come for the ritual Mom's-and-Dad's-night-out, that is what the children got.

Despite the "Why does the Jell-o always have to be green?" and "Can't we have something else?" complaints, they always got: fish sticks, frozen french fries and green Jell-o, by Robbye's definition, a "wonderful dinner."

Right after Neil moved his family into their first real home in Spartanburg, South Carolina, he called his dad, Gary.

"Guess what!" Neil said with a smirk. "All the lights are on. The refrigerator door is open. I'm running with scissors, and I'm going to sit too close to the TV."

Once in a while, our kids give us a revelation!

Carter could not get over Mary's disappointment with his Christmas gift. "They were very expensive!" he told his daughter Margaret Anne. "And she really needed them!"

"I know, Daddy," said Margaret Anne. "But it's not very romantic to give your wife a set of tires."

The image shows text "MERRY CHRISTMAS, HONEY"

DIFFERENT KINDS OF DADS

Stay-at-Home Dads

So why do they do it? Inquirers really want to know. Stay-at-home dads usually cite economics. Whoever has the best salary or benefits gets to work. (The other one comes cheaper than a day care center.) But these dads generally add their desire to be more a part of their children's lives than their own fathers were. On the other hand, most seem surprised when the stress level matches or exceeds their former "real" jobs.

Scott, an engineer turned part-time consultant, has taken on two charges, whom he calls his "twins"—a 2-year-old daughter and an 80-year-old mother-in-law.

He admits he had never been trained in pediatrics or geriatrics. "I'd go in to work for stress relief."

While working at his computer, Scott agreed to hold his infant, Nicole, when Mom was busy.

His home office was hot, and he began to sweat. In fact, the entire front of his shirt was wet.

Uh, oh, maybe Nicole's diaper was leaking.

Nope. No diaper!

For Scott, the only unpleasant part of being a dad is diaper changing. The first one he tried was at the hospital with the help of nurses. "It was the mother of all poopies," he recalls, "and I have a weak stomach."

From that day on, he gets the dry heaves every time.

One day, he heard Nicole making a "baaah-ing" sound. What was that all about?

Oh, he soon realized, she was mimicking his heaves.

Having given up his law practice, Keith from Rock Hill, South Carolina, has been a Mr. Mom for three years. In his case, as he says, "A psychiatrist trumps a lawyer." His daughters are 2 and 8. Later, Keith hopes to teach school.

When asked why, he said, "Well, I figured that, if I can teach one child and prevent him from become a lawyer, I will have done my job."

He told a reporter, "At home, I deal with infantile behavior, screaming and yelling, and a lot of poop on the side." He grinned, "Being an attorney was not such bad preparation."

Keith admits he's not much of a cook. His older daughter Kathleen confirms it. As a first grader, she announced that her favorite food was Tuna Helper.

One night when Keith had to teach a college class, he left dinner with the sitter. Later he called Kathleen and asked, "Did you have a good supper?"

"No," said Kathleen. "We ate what you fixed."

When I called Keith to find out what it's like being the stay-at-home dad of a 2-year-old, he was naming some song titles from their favorite videotape, *It's Potty Time*.* Before he could get out "Super Duper Pooper" and sing "On Top of Your Potty" (to the tune of "On Top of Old Smokey"), Kara had asked to speak to Mommy, gotten entwined in a belt on a riding toy, removed safey caps from the electrical outlet, scratched her cornea, and choked on her boo-boo bunny.

He had to excuse himself.

* See pages 92 & 93 to learn the inside story about this award-winning tape and the song composer, Loonis McGlohon.

At first, Allan cut his five-day work week to four to help Nancy with their newborn twins, Sarah and Will.

Both babies had reflux problems and required more than average care. Later, he switched to part-time.

When Nancy went back to work part-time, Allen opted to be the full-time sleepless parent, a serious long-term commitment, though he knew it wouldn't be easy.

His "awakening" came the afternoon Nancy came home to find Sarah screaming at her highest pitch.

Allan was seated on the floor holding Will, who was competing in volume. "I had wiped, burped and fed," Allan recalled, "Tears were running down *my* face, too."

Nancy immediately offered to help and rushed off for a requested burp cloth.

"A bib!" Allan wheezed loudly, putting the cloth to use.

Bib in hand, he soon sent her back for a toy.

As Nancy returned with multiple toys, Allan again spoke loud enough to be heard over two howling babies. "Get me the leather pouch under my side of the bed."

Nancy dutifully turned toward their room. Halfway there, she stopped in her tracks. "That's not funny!"

He had just asked for his gun.

George, who quit his job as a manager of supply distribution for a large hospital, claims to be master of the playground. From a chair behind the swings, he can push James, 3, Molly, 2, and Abby, 11 months, all at once. He does admit that his first week at home was a "killer." Not only was he coping with three kids but with the stitches from his vasectomy.

Stepfathers

Buddy's mom Theresa would soon be marrying Bart.

Someone asked Buddy, 9, "What do you think about having a new dad?"

"I think it's great!" he said, beaming. "I get a dad and TWO DOGS!"

FOBs & FOGs

When a child marries, the limelight beams on dad as well as the bride and groom.

As the father of the bride (FOB):

Everyone knows that the father of the bride's main function is to write checks. But "women's lib" really changed things, making his job much more difficult. In the old days, he only had to memorize two words. Now he no longer can say, "I do," he has to say, "Her mother and I do." And sometimes it comes out, "Her father and I do" or "My mother and I do."

At Bernard's daughter's wedding, the preacher asked, "Who gives this man to be married to this woman?"

Startled, Bernard answered, "His mother and I do."

At the rehearsal, the minister asked, "Who gives this woman..."

John, the bride's father responded, "Her mother, Wachovia Bank and I do."

During the wedding breakfast, Penn, the father of the bride, publicly reminded the couple that "there's a very short period between 'I do' and 'you better.'"

At a huge Jewish wedding in a prestigious Washington D.C. hotel, the fire alarm sounded during the ceremony. Someone soon discovered that chafing dish fuel lighted beneath a sensor had set off the alarm.

But before the cause was determined, the manager over-reacted, calling for an evacuation. The guests panicked, and the father of the bride wet his pants.

A minister could think of nothing more meaningful than to officiate at his only daughter's wedding. Understandably, he was nervous.

He had already made one mistake when he looked out toward the congregation and said, "I hope you'll understand if I become a little emotional. I never thought I'd be preaching at my daughter's funeral."

At an elegant, extravagant reception at the Tavern on the Green in New York's Central Park, the father of the bride called a waiter over. More filet of tenderloin? No, he had a hankering for something else.

The tuxedoed waiter rushed out to a street vendor and returned with two hot dogs.

Quentin was walking his youngest daughter, Jill, down the aisle when a grandson shouted from his pew, "Why is Gramps marrying her? He already has a wife!"

It was to have been a grand Texas outdoor wedding, but torrents drove everyone inside. The embarrassing part was that Doug, the father of the bride, was the local TV weatherman.

This Tennessee father of the bride not only paid for the wedding; he provided the location—asked his boss to let them use his place of business on a weekend. It was quite logical really. The organ there was finer than the one at their church. And the funeral chapel was brand new.

"We just prayed that nobody would die," recalled the bride.

Dick's children were quite spread out in age. The youngest was barely old enough to be her sister's flower girl. At the rehearsal, Baby Ann did fine, but there was no crowd.

Titters from both sides followed Dick's trek down the aisle. He clumped bravely along with his oldest daughter on his left arm and the youngest clamped firmly around his right leg.

Where, please, did the best man find a white satin tuxedo? His all-white outfit matched the bride's, while the groom wore his full-dress military uniform. Probably no one noticed anyway.

The father of the bride gave her away in jeans, a checked flannel shirt and tennis shoes.

Henry presented his daughter to her groom and turned to join his wife. But his foot twisted awkwardly on the bride's train. He stepped back to catch himself on the corner of the pew, overturning it with a crash.

A cacophony followed. He had also dumped the mother of the bride and the noisy contents of her purse onto the floor in a crumpled, crunching heap.

Never mind that the wedding was held in a fine Baptist church in Columbia, South Carolina. Captain Telegram appeared anyway, with his blue cape, his engineer's hat, balloons and a diaper with a giant pin.

During the solemn vows, he strode down the aisle, grabbed the bride by the waist and began singing his telegram.

Wouldn't you think the father of the bride would knock him flat? No indeed. He hired the guy.

Although wealthy, Don had insisted that his daughter's reception be held in the Washington & Lee alumni house. Those who knew how notoriously tight he was were not surprised.

But a befuddled guest, thinking it was the family home, went to make a telephone call and found only a pay phone. Fuming, he returned to say, "I knew Don was cheap, but I didn't think he'd go this far!"

The band leader for the New York reception insisted on being paid in cash. That's why Ira, the bride's father, had $5,000 in his inside coat pocket.

As the evening wore on and the music heated up, he took off his coat and draped it onto the back of his chair. Surprise! When he went to pay the band, no money!

Several weeks later, after the bride and groom returned from their honeymoon, the two families gathered to watch the wedding videos.

One camera had been set up to record the action at the head table. Ira's abandoned coat hung on the chair in plain view. A figure appeared, and a hand slipped inside the pocket to remove the cash. There was no doubt who it was: the father of the groom!

As the father of the groom (FOG):

Eli's troubles began before the wedding. He got arrested at the bachelor party the night before. Well, he wasn't the only one. So did both his sons, including the groom. Seems the neighbors from the apartment complex, where the party was held, complained.

Unfortunately, a party-goer, who tends to talk ugly when drunk, had been the first to exchange words with the officers. The confrontation became louder than the music.

To find out what was going on, Eli stepped outside with a drink in his hand. The next thing he knew, he was hand-cuffed and in the back of the police car.

The groom came out and ended up in the same squad car. His brother drove up about that time. A photographer by trade, he saw the humor of the situation and got out his camera. While he was snapping photos of their predicament, a fed-up policeman arrested him for obstructing justice.

Eli had to call his wife to come down to the station to bail them out. Problem was: it took cash. She didn't keep enough laying around the house to bail out three family members. And so, she thought of the one person she knew who not only might have some cash in his pocket but who would think it really important to have her three men available the next morning.

Before dawn, Eli and his sons were bailed out by the father of the bride, a teetotaller.

As he faced his bride to repeat the vows, Thomas broke down. No words, only tears came out. Five minutes of crying was too long, especially for Warren, his old man. Both father and son were military men, and everyone knows that this breed doesn't show emotion.

Warren stood it as long as he could. Then he strode to the front. "Suck it up, son," he ordered.

Son sucked.

GRANDDADDYHOOT

What is it about grandfathers? Even the gruffest of guys (in the public's eyes) or the strictest disciplinarian (in his children's eyes) becomes a playful pussycat with his grandchildren.

When Chas wanted to ride on Grandy's back, Grandy complained that Chas, 4, had grown too heavy to ride piggyback and Grandy's back was too old.

"Pop Pop lets me ride on *his* back," said Chas of his other grandfather.

Suddenly, Chas wasn't too heavy at all. Not that day, nor the rest of the summer. And that horsie could gallop, too!

Fred was sitting in his Kingman, Arizona, church with his grandchild, Natasha.

"Papa, I'm hungry," she said.

He just shook his head.

But Natasha was not to be denied. "But Jesus said if you come, He would feed all of us."

Fred got up and brought back a pack of crackers.

Sometimes Grandpa gets frustrated.

Grandma and Granddad were baby-sitting with Buddy, while their daughter was at work. Granddad was supposed to be cleaning out the vacuum cleaner. Somehow he got side-tracked by a football game on TV in the playroom.

That's when Grandma heard the sound of a brook. Unnoticed, Buddy had put the vacuum cleaner hose into the washing machine, sucking out all the water. By the time they could stop him, the laundry room *and* the playroom floors were a soapy lake.

That marked the first day Buddy was ever sent to his room!

"That man is bothering me!" cried Meredith in a store.

Customers and the manager came running. Meredith's mother was nowhere in sight.

Charles, the older man she was fingering, sputtered and turned red. Then he began laughing until he cried.

Charles was Meredith's grandfather.

Allison, 5, loved to ride in her grandfather's old VW "Beetle." One day, the two of them were in it, when Allison urged, "Faster, Papa! Faster!"

He complied.

"Faster, Papa! Faster!" she said again.

He loved to please the apple of his eye.

But when he returned her to her mother, Allison cried, "Mama! Papa SPEEDS!"

Grandmas aren't the only ones who think grandchildren say the cutest things.

Bill's second grandchild was due soon. Before the Big Event, he asked Alexis, 4, "What are you going to name the baby?"

"Moses."

"Oh, where'd you find Moses?"

"Grandpa," she said with an exasperated tone, "you can find him in any Bible book."

At a Peak Experience concession in Richmond, Virginia, Scottie, 5, and his grandfather Frank were waiting for his older sister to finish scaling the rock wall.

Scottie turned to Frank. "Dandaddy, what's my phone number?"

Dandaddy told him. And moments later, the child was repeating it to the attractive young woman in charge and adding, "If you ever want to talk, call me."

Frank was amused at his grandson's maleness. "That's what I was going to say!"

During a wedding ceremony, the flower girl called out, "Wake up, Paw Paw!"

Granddad was praying.

"What happens when you die?" asked 5-year old James.

To answer without getting into long, possibly scary physiological and/or theological explanations, Lisa told him that death happens when the body stops working, just like when a battery runs out in a toy, and the toy can no longer work.

A few weeks later, during dinner, Lisa happily announced that his grandfather, George, was going to retire.

"What does 'retire' mean?" James wanted to know.

"Papa will stop working."

James burst into tears. "I don't want Papa to die!"

A Wyckoff, New Jersey, mom, Athena told Jeffrey that Papou, his grandfather, had to go to the dentist.

Jeffrey, 3, knew why: "His tooth broke because he talks too much."

"Bubba, guess what?" said Hailey, 3, while the family was eating in a restaurant in Greenville, South Carolina.

"What?" said the grandfather, who expected to be called "Bubbadaddy" but found himself cheerfully answering to "Bubba."

"I'm not supposed to say 'dammit,'" she said.

Her mother, Ashley, spoke right up. "Hailey, you're not supposed to say that word."

Hailey frowned. "Why not? You say 'dammit.'"

Grandfather to Multitudes

A grandfather of seven, Loonis, a musician who has played and composed for many internationally-known singers over five decades, was asked to write the songs for a videotape. Fatherhood and grandfatherhood prepared him for the project called *It's Potty Time.*

After it was produced, a fellow musician remarked, "You know, Loonis, of all the wonderful songs you've composed, you may be best known for those."

True, those tunes have been translated into Spanish, sung on David Letterman and other talk shows and named one of the Ten Top Cult Videos.

"My daughter said she wished I had never made that video," he said. "because my grandson had to mimic the dialog every time."

For instance, the mother in the video asks, "Did you remember to wash your hands?" and the little boy runs back in the bathroom and does that. Loonis's grandson Edward regularly insisted that he—and she—play out the whole scenario.

I asked Loonis McGlohon for permission to show you why his songs are so popular. Here are my favorites:

Super Duper Pooper

I am a super duper pooper.
I can potty with the best.
No more diapers to get in my way.
I bet you are impressed.
I am a super duper pooper.
I know when I have to go.
I'll take a bow, I'm a big kid now,
I'm the best pooper you know.

Reproduced through the courtesy of Learning Through Education, owner of the video, *It's Potty Time.*

On Top of Your Potty
(Mother sings to the tune of "On Top of Old Smokey")

On top of your potty
You're sitting to go.
Oh, life is much better
Without diapers below.
But you must be patient,
So sit there and smile
But instead of waiting
Why not rest for awhile?

Reproduced through the courtesy of Learning Through Education, owner of the video, *It's Potty Time*.

DaddyHoot

Tips
for
Sanity

ADVICE
BASED ON ANECDOTES
OF ACTUAL EVENTS
IN THIS BOOK

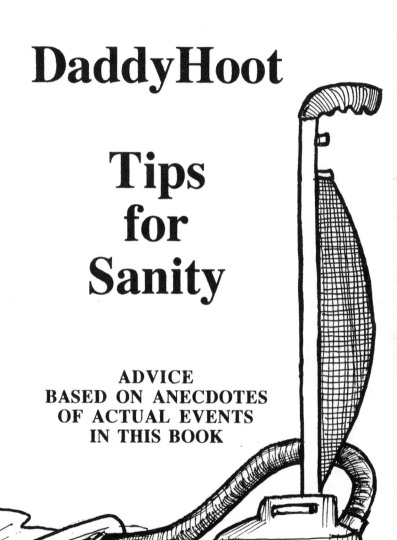

DaddyHoot
TIPS FOR SANITY

From conception through grandfatherhood...

* Always have damp baby wipes—for yourself.

During pregnancy...

* Be forewarned: Pregnancy lasts eight months and then a year.

* Stick around, no matter how irritating or irritable she gets; she'll appreciate you later.

* Never compare her to a VW beetle or her maternity panties to a car cover.

* When you're racing to the hospital, be sure she's in the car.

At the actual event...

* Don't offer to call the plumber when her water breaks.

* Let the *doctor* declare the sex. (But even *he* may be wrong.)

When your children are babies...

* Choke back every sign of laughter when your child spits up on or sprays your wife's face.

* It's fruitless to try to fool the baby into thinking you're Mom by wearing her bathrobe.

* It's okay to be germ-paranoid with your first; but by the third one, it's okay to stop by the mall on the way home from the hospital—or drop by your office to show her off.

* Be certain you know how to spell the baby's name before you have a bracelet engraved for the new mom.

* If your crawler doesn't respond to your "no," record Mom's voice saying it to use when she's not around.

While they are in the "terrible twos"...

* Never take a child in training pants into a store that sells potty seats.

* For great results, learn to sing Loonis McGlohon's "Super Duper Pooper" song.

* Among their very first words will be the bad ones you know you shouldn't use.

* Pray that the bad word he just learned will come out "truck" when he says it at church.

* If you take your son squirrel hunting, don't hold him on one shoulder while you shoot with the other hand—the "boom" will trigger his bladder.

When they are still young...

* Avoid telling a child something you don't want quoted to a teacher, preacher or shoe salesman.

* Never leave a kid in a car alone or he may practice driving without you.

* If he spills milk, don't console him by showing how much fun it is to slurp the milk off the table with a straw.

* Don't scrimp on hiring a babysitter while your boss or other important people are visiting or your daughter may dance into the room naked or your son might fill all the guests' cars with "gas" from the garden hose.

* When your son announces to everyone in the grocery store that you "peed" in the sink, keep in mind that he has never seen a urinal.

* Watch what you eat—that cauliflower just might be Pla-Doh.

* Be sure know know the difference between a dress and a slip before you dress your daughters for church.

* If you shave off your moustache, don't be offended if your kids don't recognize you.

* If you forget to keep one eye on your little one at church, at least try to read your wife's lips in the choir.

* Never let kids of any age outnumber you.

As they grow older...

* When you're leading a Boy Scout troop on a hike, be sure you know where you're going.

* After making a "pit stop" on a long interstate trip, always count heads before getting too far down the highway.

* Be appreciative if your child shouts in public what everyone else is thinking but doesn't have the nerve to say.

* No matter how bad your allergy is, don't ever ask your kids to choose between you and a pet.

* If you threaten military school, let them think you're taking them there to scare them into promising goodness forever.

* Avoid doing anything against the law that includes your child, because she might want to go to jail with you.

* If you're caught telling a lie or cussing, you must submit to the same punishment you would give them.

As they're figuring out what birds & bees do...

* Unless you want your kids to think you haven't a clue about the facts of life, don't answer their questions with "Tell me what you already know."

* Admit to your children that, yes, you and Mom did that TWICE.

* Better not make the description of sex too interesting, or they may ask to watch next time.

ADULT TREE

* You need not correct him, if your youngster thinks the seventh commandment says "Don't cut adult trees."

* Keep your cool when you tell the children that they will soon have a new sister, and one admits thinking you were "too old to do that."

When they are "trying teens"...

* When you discover a pile of ice in the backyard after you were away on weekend trip, don't believe your teenagers' tale about a freak hailstorm while you were gone.

* Try not to get angry at your wife if she advises your daughter to mention marijuana before telling about the speeding ticket so you'll be relieved when she admits teasing about the drug.

* Take seriously the teenager who threatens to run away—if she packs the teddy bear she can't sleep without.

* The more you criticize your daughter's boyfriend, the more she'll adore him, so let her grandmother send him away.

* Don't tell your teenager what you already know about his behavior; let him think you know more.

If they try to pull a ridiculous role reversal on you...

* Agree with your preschooler when, at the hardware store, he reminds you, "That's a *want*, not a *need*."

* Believe her when your daughter advises you that it's not very romantic to give your wife a set of tires for Christmas.

* Do as you're told when your son says, "Be a man, Dad! Go on by yourself!"

* Okay, admit it: your daughters have been telling you where to go for years.

* Pull a role reversal of your own: when the kids insist on buying heavily-advertised kiddie cereal, trash the contents and substitute dog food.

* Don't be surprised when your adult children get the first place of their own if they break all your rules about keeping all the lights on and leaving the refrigerator door open (until they get the electric bill).

If you're a stay-at-home dad...

* Appreciate your preparation in the business world for dealing with all the infantile behavior, screaming and yelling and a lot of poop on the side.

If you're a new step dad...

* It's okay if he's more excited about getting your dogs.

If you're a father of multiples...

* "If it's quiet, he's busy" applies twofold or threefold.

* Forget the cabinet lock idea, as two or three working together can master one in a heartbeat.

* If you take your toddler twins golfing, don't leave them in the golf cart to drive alone. (Duh!)

* When you get tired of people asking if they're all really yours, say, "Yes, but..." and name multiple mamas.

* Be aware that, when your quads turn teen, you will be considered four times as dumb.

As a grandpa...

* If the *other* grandfather gives "horsie" rides, you do, too —and show how you can gallop.

* When your grandchild compares you with Jesus, be *extra* kind and generous.

* Beware if your grandkid encourages you to go faster when you're driving. (She may just want to report your speeding.)

* Remember, if your little grandson offers a beautiful stranger his phone number, he may be taking after you.

* If your granddaughter says "Wake up, Paw Paw" when you're praying at a wedding, you need to see that she goes to church more often.

* Blame yourself if your grandchild blames his parent when he gets reprimanded for saying the "D" word; YOU raised that parent.

* When a little one suggests that Grandpa broke his tooth "because he talks too much," you probably do.

MY DAD, THE STORYTELLER

When I was growing up, fathers were the bread-winners; mothers, the child-raisers. Daddy was often away on business, and it was not unusual to see him on week-ends only, whether we were at home or at the beach all summer.

We loved each other, but had very little in common to talk about. I did enjoy his stories, generally told over dinner to company. Whenever we had new guests, he would tell his old favorite tales.

Only after Mother died did I really get to know my dad. I wanted him to tape some of those stories about his traveling salesman days in the West and the wacky, wonderful and downright weird people he met there.

After a slow start, my husband wisely said, "He needs an audience." I agreed, and so we began a four-year process of his taping and my writing what became the book, *Only Forty Miles of Pavement*, his traveling salesman experiences from oil boom days through the Depression. His first territory in the Panhandle of Texas and Western Oklahoma had 19,000 square miles in 19 counties and only 40 miles of paved roads. "And that included the main streets of the towns," he always added.

Mid-book, we re-traveled much of that first territory to "check memories." For him, it was the first time back in over 50 years. For me, it was like entering his past literally — actually seeing the terrain and places he knew and even hearing some of his tales retold from someone else's point of view.

We made other research trips to Oklahoma City and Kansas City. In Chicago, we searched for Al Capone's first headquarter-hotel, where Daddy had innocently spent a night, and enjoyed red-carpet treatment from the president of the company that never promoted him past district manager.

When we turned on the tape recorder the first time, I thought I had "heard 'em all." Not only was I mistaken; I was wrong a hundred times over. But it was a good kind of wrong to be. For through our process together, I really got to know my father. We became closer than we had ever been in our lives. This I treasure. This kind of relationship I would wish for every daughter and her father.

THINGS I LEARNED FROM MY DAD

* Fathers make all the major family decisions, like when we move to another house (not necessarily where) or whether we can afford another car (not what model). Mothers make all the rest.

* A dad must set a good example for his children. That's why, when I left for college, he asked Mother, "Does this mean I no longer have to eat carrots?"

* Dessert consists of anything that has ice cream on it, under it or in it.

* Bad drivers are always "damned women drivers," even if they are bald and have beards.

* Christmas gifts for your spouse should be romantic remembrances, like a set of new tires.

* Truth is essential, so never ever ever ever ever ever ever say you'll "never" do something. (His follow-up reasoning: "Never is a very long time.")

* A negative attitude, unappetizing dinner or dull company can be instantly transformed with a humorous story.

Other Humor Titles
by A. Borough Books

If you enjoyed this book, you're sure to like:

MotherHoot - The Lighter Side of Motherhood
True anecdotes about moms from pregnancy through grandmotherhood
+ MotherHoot Tips for Sanity
Margaret G. Bigger   Cartoons by Loyd Dillon
ISBN 0-9640606-8-X
Standard print - 1999, 2nd Printing 1999 Paperback pp. 128 $9.95

MEN! Cry Flustered Frustrated Females Everywhere
True MALE TALES, GIVENS & HOW COMES from 44 of those FFFs
proving that typical men don't think/act/talk like typical females.
Margaret G. Bigger   Cartoons by Loyd Dillon
ISBN 1-893597-01-6
LARGE PRINT - 2000   Paperback pp. 96 $7.50

Churchgoers' Chuckles
True Tales - You Can't Make This Stuff Up! Anecdotes from 97
churchgoers in 16 denominations and 30 states.
Margaret G. Bigger   Cartoons by Loyd Dillon
ISBN 1-893597-02-4
LARGE PRINT - 2000   Paperback pp. 96 $7.50

Kitties & All That Litter
Mewsings, GRRRoaners, true cat tales and kitty limericks by 26 cat-
loving curmudgeons.
Edited/Curtailed by Margaret G. Bigger Cat-tooned by Loyd Dillon
ISBN 1-893597-00-8
LARGE PRINT - 1999   Paperback pp. 96 $7.50

You've GOT to Have a Sense of Humor to Have a
Wedding Humorous, outrageous & disastrous true tales from the
engagement through the honeymoon + advice not found in wedding guides.
Margaret G. Bigger   Cartoons by Loyd Dillon
ISBN 0-9640606-5-5
Standard print - 1997, 3rd Printing 1998 Paperback pp. 128 $9.95

Gray-Haired Grins & Giggles

Guess What! Grammy & Grandy have a sense of humor, too! True tales
from childhood to retirement by 45 senior authors
Margaret G. Bigger   Cartoons by Loyd Dillon
ISBN 0-9640606-3-9
Standard print - 1995, 4th Printing 1996 Paperback pp. 128 $12.95
ISBN 0-9640606-7-1
LARGE PRINT - 1998, somewhat abridged Paperback pp.140 $13.95

You Can Tell You're a Charlottean If...

288 ways that residents (natives, newcomers and long-timers) of Charlotte,
NC are different from the rest of the world + Head Scratchers & Queenz
Quiz. 91 locals contributed lines.
Margaret Bigger & Betsy Webb   Cartoons by Loyd Dillon
ISBN 0-9640606-6-3
LARGE PRINT - 1998   Paperback pp. 96 $7.95

You Know You're In Charlotte If...

Current residents, former Charlotteans, even outsiders contributed lines to
show the uniqueness of Charlotte + cute & clever business names &
license plates, Charlotte celebrities & Local Sports History Quiz.
90 locals contributed lines.
ISBN 1-893597-03-2
Margaret G. Bigger   Cartoons by Loyd Dillon
LARGE PRINT - 2000   Paperback pp. 96 $7.95

What's Next?

TeacherHoot - The Lighter Side of Teaching
Puppies & All That Waggin'
Kitties & All That Litter, Vol. II
MEN! WOMEN!
Churchgoers' Chuckles, Vol. II
ParentHoot - The Lighter Side of Parenthood
But Not for Lunch - The Lighter Side of Retirement

MORE ON NEXT PAGE

Other books of true-experience anecdotes by A B B :

World War II: It Changed Us Forever
From the battlefront to the homefront and places in between.
33 authors tell it like it was! 93 tales. Vintage photos.
Standard print-1994. 3rd printing-2001   Paperback   140 pp. $12.95
ISBN:0-9640606-0-4
Edited by Margaret G. Bigger

The Great Depression: How We Coped, Worked and Played - True stories written by the people who lived them.
A joint project of A. Borough Books and The Museum of the New South.
Pub. Date: September, 2001
ISBN:1-893597-04-0
Edited by Margaret G. Bigger

Bigger's guide to recording memoirs:

Recalling Your Memories on Paper, Tape or Videotape - Self-help guide to preserving memoirs & photos.
Also how to help parents record memories. Excerpts from seniors'
family booklets. Vintage photos.
Standard print-1996.   Paperback   160 pp. $13.95
ISBN:0-9640606-4-7

See next page for order form.

KNOW SOMEONE WHO
COULD USE A LITTLE HUMOR?
Order humor books for gifts!
Autographed & personalized!!!

_____copies of **DaddyHoot** @ $9.95 $_____

_____copies of **MotherHoot** @ $9.95 $_____

_____copies of **MEN!** @ $7.50 $_____

_____copies of **Churchgoers' Chuckles** @ $7.50 $_____

_____copies of **Kitties & All That Litter** @ $7.50 $_____

_____copies of **You've GOT to Have a Sense of**
Humor to Have a Wedding @ $9.95 $_____

_____copies of **Gray-Haired Grins & Giggles**
standard print @ $12.95 $_____
LARGE PRINT @ $13.95 $_____

_____copies of **You've Can Tell You're a**
Charlottean If...@ $7.95 $_____
_____copies of **You Know You're in**
Charlotte If...@ $7.95 $_____

Other ABB titles:
_____copies of **World War II: It Changed Us**
Forever @ $12.95 $_____
_____copies of **Recalling Your Memories on Paper,**
Tape or Videotape @$13.95 $_____
Subtotal $_____
Discount   **(20% for 10 or more)** $_____
NC residents must add 6.5% tax $_____
Postage & handling $3 for 1st 2 books
+$1 more for each multiple of 5 $_____
TOTAL $_____

Please complete this form on the back.

Name_____

Address_____

City, State, Zip_____

Phone #_____

Specify here how you want your books to be personalized:

DaddyHoot book to_____
Circle: new dad   experienced dad   granddad
Names of kids_____
MotherHoot book to_____
Circle: expectant mom   mother grandmother
Names of kids_____
MEN! book to_____name of her man_____
Church book to_____denomination_____
Cat book to_____name of cat/cats_____
Wedding book to_____
Circle: bride &/or groom   mother of bride   minister/priest/rabbi
Date of wedding if known_____
Senior humor book to_____
Charlottean book to_____
Charlotte book to_____
World War II book to_____
Recalling memories guide to_____

Other instructions:

Please mail check or money order with this form to:

A. Borough Books
P.O. Box 15391
Charlotte, NC 28211

DO YOU HAVE A FUNNY STORY ABOUT BEING A PARENT OR GRANDPARENT?

Your anecdote could be in Margaret Bigger's next book ParentHoot!

Check chapter title:

____Who's Pregnant? We are!
____Who? Why?
____New Parent, New Babe, No Instructions
____Terrible—But Bearable—Twos
____Said *WHAT?*
____Did *WHAT?*
____The Parent Said *WHAT?* Did *WHAT?*
____Crime & Punishment, Kid Style
____Birds, Bees, Adult Trees & Anatomies
____Somebody Control This Child!
____Teens—Too Trying for Words
____Multiple Kids Need Multiple Parents
____You Can't Outlaw Mothers-in-Law
____There's No Such Thing as an Empty Nest
____Ridiculous Role Reversal
____GrandparentHoot
____New chapter idea: _____

Your favorite anecdote:

USE BACK OF FORM FOR MORE

More anecdotes (specify chapter titles):

Note: We will use only first names in the book, but we will notify you by postcard if your story makes the publisher's cut. Your name will be listed as a contributor.

Name_____

Address_____

City, State, Zip_____

Phone #_____

Please mail this form to: **A. Borough Books**
P.O. Box 15391
Charlotte, NC 28211

DO YOU HAVE MORE FUNNY STORIES ON OTHER TOPICS FOR FUTURE BOOKS BY MARGARET BIGGER?

_____ **TeacherHoot - The Lighter Side of Teaching**
True tales from every imaginable type of teacher,
including drivers ed instructor, college professor, adult
literacy teacher, Sunday school teacher, day care worker
+ some TeacherHoot Tips for Sanity.

_____ **Puppies & All That Waggin'**
Ponderings by puppies or their master pundits, puppy
poetry, GRRRoaners, how comes (one liners) and
some true dog tales.

_____ **Kitties & All That Litter, Vol. II**
More true cat tales, mewsings and GRRRoaners, some
kitty limericks, how comes and other one-liners.

_____ **Churchgoers' Chuckles, Vol. II**
More true tales about not-so-solemn services, what kids
thought they learned in Sunday school, children's
prayers, churchgoers' mishaps, PKs' antics, preachers'
foibles, not-so-perfect funerals or weddings.

_____ **MEN! WOMEN!**
True Male Tales & Female Tales showing the difference in
the way each thinks/acts/talks + some funny lines:
How come a man/woman...
It's a given that guys/gals...

_____ **But Not for Lunch - The Lighter Side of
Retirement** True tales from males and females, retirees
and their children + some funny lines and tips for sanity.

_____ Another collection of true wedding tales from the
engagement through the honeymoon + more advice
not found in wedding guides.

Write anecdotes here (specify which book)

Note: We will use only first names in the book, but we will notify you by postcard if your story makes the publisher's cut. Your name will be listed as a contributor.

Name_____

Address_____

City, State, Zip_____

Phone #_____

Please mail this form to: **A. Borough Books**
                               P.O. Box 15391
                               Charlotte, NC 28211